A Proud Andy holding the RLODC trophy, with brother Pete following the win over Hampshire at Lord's.

Cover photograph reproduced

courtesy of Jacob Hurry

Head Coach Jason Kerr with Andy

The photograph says it all! A jubilant Somerset team on fire in 2019

The Hurry (Ure) family crest, a lion's paw erect and erased gules, with the motto, "Sans Tache," (Without Stain) plate 120, crest 9, in "Fairbairn's crests"—Urrie, Urry and Hurry, the same being very conclusive proof that these names have all a common origin.

Erased gules is simply serrated red, as on the lion rampant. Red is one of the tinctures used in heraldry; the others being azure (blue), sable (black), vert (green) and purpure (purple).

.

"Success is not final. Failure is not fatal.

It's the courage to continue that counts"

Winston Churchill

---oOo---

Andy has dedicated this book

to his parents Helen Margaret, and John

IT'S A STATE OF MIND ©

ISBN 9781096080923

22 North Street
Wiveliscombe
Somerset
TA4 2JY

PJ Lennon

Table of Contents

During the summer of 2004 Roy Kerslake and I conducted a survey of Somerset cricket which led us to interview several of the 1st X1 and the coaching and support staff. Ricky Ponting was with us at the time and I spoke to him during the Championship game at Durham. One of his most telling comments was his obvious appreciation of the work Sarge was doing with the squad both in his then role of training the team and his pre match work in helping the coaching staff prepare the players.

The report eventually led to a shake-up of Somerset during the early part of the 2005 season and the new role of Director of Cricket coming into place, a position I was happy to take accept. I immediately put into place several initiatives Roy and I thought could take the club forward including revamping the development pathway and the coaching methods.

Towards the end of that season Mark Garraway was appointed to the England support staff and the position of coach became vacant. Andy by that time was doing some work in the Middle East and one of the first contacts I made was to pull him back for a first interview. I never got to interview anybody else as during our conversations his ideas and the disciplined approach to his methods dovetailed into what I wanted to bring to Somerset. He got the job on the spot! It also combined with the signing of Justin Langer as an overseas player for a brief but telling period during the 2006 season during which JL told me at Guildford that "Sarge" was one of the best coaches he had ever worked with. They were to combine during the 2007 season as captain and coach and lead us through an unforgettable championship season where 12 victories took us through to promotion into the 1st division. Although disappointments were come in not securing 1-day finals wins and the agonising day at Durham when we finished level on points with Notts but lost the championship on count back he has now rectified that with a fabulous 1 Day Cup victory at Lords as Director of Cricket in company with Jason Kerr as Coach. These two were the bedrock of my days as DoC and now as President with Sarge as DoC and Jason as Coach and with several of the younger players that we brought through the development programme heady days are back at the County Ground.

Brian Rose

President: Somerset County Cricket Club

---o0o---

In a few words, Andy Hurry is one of the best and most inspirational people I have met in my cricketing life.

When Brian Rose first rang me offering me a six-week stint at the Somerset County Cricket Club I nearly fell off my seat. Having just been knocked out on the first ball of my 100th Test match in Johannesburg, I was at home in Perth contemplating retirement and recovering from the blow to my head from

Makhaya Ntini. Brian's call surprised me because most of the time was to be taken up playing 20/20 cricket, with two first-class games thrown in. As a Test opening batsman, I wasn't necessarily synonymous with T20 cricket. After picking myself up from the ground and accepting the Club's proposal I arrived at Taunton to be greeted by the steely-eyed Andy "Sarge' Hurry who offered me a coffee and a chat. This would be the first of some 1000 coffees and chats we shared together.

Instantly his honesty and vision for the Club were apparent and I couldn't wait to get to work with him. Not only is Sarge honest, meticulous in his preparation and relentless in his work ethic, but his loyalty is a trait I will always treasure. He and Darren Veness helped me overcome a problem I had had with a stalker in England

and from that day on we have all been friends for life. Sarge is a man I respect deeply and a person I would go to war with any day of the week. I can give no greater compliment.

Justin Langer: Head Coach - Australian Men's Cricket Team

I was in the UAE with England playing Pakistan in the ODI & T20 and I was looking for a new coach to join us in the UAE in order to give another coach a break from touring. I'd heard some positive things about Andy from talking to various people in the game and Gordon Lord Head of Elite Coaching at the ECB (England and Wales Cricket Board) suggested Andy Hurry.

I trusted Gordon's judgment so I invited Andy out and he was dead keen to come; as soon as he arrived in our group, he made a positive difference. Everything about him suggested discipline, hard work but also a bit of fun. He definitely has a glint in his eye and he likes a bit of fun but he is a man who is serious about competition and winning and getting things done and he projects these messages so powerfully.

I remember I was introducing him to the management team and I think I said something like; "this is Andy Hurry and he was an instructor in the Army". He stopped me straight away and looked me straight in the eye and said; "...excuse me for interrupting but I would prefer it if you didn't say that I was in the army, I was in the

Marines and there's a big difference..." I don't think I shall ever forget that piercing look!

I really liked that feeling of the positive influence that oozed out of him and it was obvious that he could handle himself, so I threw him into the deep end and asked him to run fielding practice next day, which would have been his first full day with us.

He had prepared impeccably and he ran it beautifully. He is -any man's equal but don't try to fool him. Andy chooses his friends very carefully but when you become his friend, you are his friend for life.

I consider it an honour to be included in that select group of people. I am delighted that he has accepted the role of Director of Cricket at his beloved Somerset and I predict continuing success for an impressive man.

Andy Flower

Director of England Cricket

There are indeed two 5 o'clocks in every day, as is sensitively pointed out by the Royal Marines in their 'Royal Marines Forum' and on that first morning of training in October 1989, Andy and his fellow recruits would have had their first rude awakening by the drill instructor.

The son of a Catholic mother from Dundee, in Scotland. His father, the son of a sheep and poultry farmer from Busselton, southwest of Perth, Western Australia, Andy was a determined young man and he knew what he wanted to do from a young age; "School got in the way of playing sport" is Andy's tongue in cheek reference to his lifetime love of all sports. He will readily admit that he has a selfish drive in him but it's clear from our conversations that he doesn't lack empathy for other people. It is perhaps a coincidence that both of Andy's parents came from very close to Perth, albeit on opposite sides of the world.

Andy's father was a passionate sportsman and played football all weekend, mornings and afternoons and as winter drew to a close and spring became summer, on would go the cricket whites and he'd spend the weekends morning and afternoon on the square or in the pavilion.

Andy acquired his father's burning passion for sport, saying; "I just used to follow him around and watch him play football and cricket from as far back I can remember." It was pretty obvious that Andy had inherited his father's enthusiasm for the game and that in 1983 he was already being touted as a cricketer of some note. There is no doubt that he had ample talent, enough to stand shoulder to shoulder with other emerging talents at the time.

---o0o---

Acknowledgements

The author would sincerely like to thank the following people for the generosity of their time in the research of this book.

- Peter Hurry, brother of Andy
- Amy Blythe, Andy's partner
- Jacob, Andy's son
- Brian Rose, Somerset CCC President
- Andy Flower, England Head Coach and ECB Director of Cricket
- Vic Marks, TMS commentator, former Somerset
C   CC cricket Chairman and ex-Somerset and England off-break bowler,
- Guy Lavender, former CEO of Somerset CCC, now CEO of the MCC at Lord's
- Marcus Trescothick, ex England Cricket captain, ex-Somerset CCC Captain, record run scorer for Somerset CCC having scored 50 centuries.
- Andrew Caddick, ex England explosive fast bowler and helicopter pilot
- Jason Kerr, Head Coach at Somerset CCC
- Lewis Gregory, T20 captain 2018 season
- Polly Rhodes, Somerset Scorer, for her excellent work in proof-reading and offering her expertise.
- Mick Hill, Andy's PTI Instructor
- Richard Gould, Surrey Cricket Chief Executive
- Brian Rose, President of Somerset CCC
- Fraser Day, Former Royal Marines colleague

- Justin Langer, Record-breaking Australian Cricketer
- Kevin Shine, Former SCCC Head Coach and current ECB fast bowling National Skills Head Coach
- Tom Abell, Somerset CCC captain
- Andy Nash, Entrepreneur, Former Chair of Somerset CCC, for his invaluable help in the original formation of the book and solid advice,
- Chris Slocombe OBE, Former Royal Marines, Royal Navy and Combined Services Cricketer Commander Piers Moore, Former Royal Navy and Combined Services Cricketer
- Sarah Trunks, Commercial Manager
- Richard Walsh, his twitter name @richardscoop sums him up.
- Gordon Lord, ex ECB Elite Coaching Mentor and Coach Educator
- Gary Naylor, Book and Theatre critic and Guerrilla cricket commentator.
- To the various unnamed members of Somerset CCC staff, without whose help and support this book would not have been possible,
- To everybody at 10Radio in the lovely town of Wiveliscombe, without whom I would never have achieved my dream of becoming a journalist and subsequently an author.
- Lastly, my sincere thanks go to my partner, Wilma, for her endless patience, unwavering support and for just being there.

----o0o----

St. Mary's Church Busselton, Western Australia
Photograph reproduced courtesy of ©The State Library of Western Australia - 2003

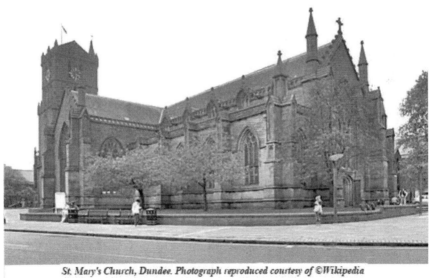

St. Mary's Church, Dundee. Photograph reproduced courtesy of ©Wikipedia

Chapter 1

In the Beginning

Chapter 1

In the Beginning

Andy Hurry, 'Sarge' to his colleagues, was born on the 15th October 1964 in Bushey Maternity Hospital, Heathbourne Road, Bushey Heath, Bushey, Hertfordshire. The maternity dept. operated as an independent unit until 1977, when it was moved and incorporated into the Edgware General Hospital. He lived with his mother and father in Harrow approximately 6 miles from Bushey.

Ask a representative sample of people what they

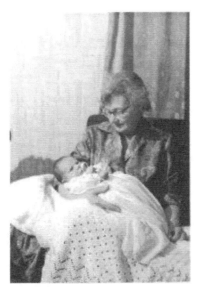

New-born Andy with his Grandmother

associate with the word 'Harrow' and it's a fair bet that most of them will answer; "Harrow Public School".

There has been a school at Harrow as early as 1527, as alluded to in *A History of the County of Middlesex: Volume 4*. "Richard Gerard, who entered Caius (Gonville and Caius) College, Cambridge, in 1567, attended a school at Harrow, and a letter of 1626 mentioned one there as early as Mary's reign [18 February 1516 – 17 November 1558]". [1]

The Harrow School uniform still includes a black tie, which as local legend says, the boys had to wear at the time of the death of Queen Victoria and the order has "never been rescinded". [2]

Soon Bury St. Edmunds in Suffolk beckoned and in 1967, Andy's parents moved there from Harrow. When he was four, Andy's mother gave birth to Peter, his younger brother. Andy doesn't remember his mother being pregnant but he does remember being 'shipped out' one day and returning to find his baby brother, Peter snuggled in his mother's arms!

Andy's Mum and Dad, Helen and John were both thoughtful and private people and Helen, through reasons of her own, was reluctant to share her early life with her family and Andy only discovered more about her young life after her death, at the age of 83 in March 2017 following a short battle with cancer.

Andy's partner Amy talks affectionately about the various conversations she and Helen had and comments that Helen was indeed circumspect with respect to her young life but Amy was full of admiration for Helen and enjoyed tremendously their time together.

◆ ◆ ◆

Andy with Mum Helen

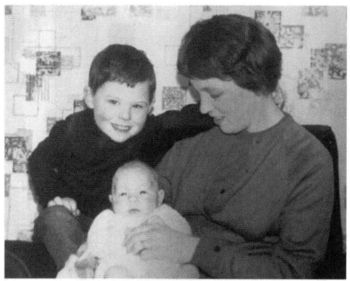

A beaming Andy with his Mum and new baby brother Peter

The Perth Royal Infirmary, in the 1930s Reproduced courtesy of ©Tour Scotland

She was born Helen Margaret O'Neill in Longforgan, Dundee, to parents John O'Neill and Helen Margaret née Stewart. Helen Margaret Stewart gave birth to her daughter at 9.50 pm on 6th September 1933 in what is now the Perth Royal Infirmary in Tibbermore.

The Domesday Book contains a mention of Longforgan. St Modwenna, who died in 521, is believed to have founded a church there and, it was said, was a disciple of St Patrick.

It is alleged that Sir Patrick Gray, Baron of Longforgan, held '…a baronial court…' there in 1385 on the Longforgan or Hund Hill.

The village was created a burgh of barony in 1672.[3] Castle Huntly, established in the 14th century and further developed in the 17th and 18th centuries, is located half a mile south-west of the village.[4] It is now an open prison, housing 285 low risk adult prisoners.

During her pregnancy, Helen Stewart and John lived for just over 4 months at Hilton Farm in Craigend, Perth. However, at the time of Andy's mother Helen's birth they were living at Rawes Farm in Longforgan, a distance of a little under 18 miles from Craigend.

John, the 30-year-old cattleman and Helen, the 20 year-old nursemaid married on the 26th May 1933 at the parish church of Dunbarney, which is just over a mile from Craigend, southwest of Perth, Scotland. Meanwhile, on the 5th September 1931, 33-year-old Funeral director Sydney Alfred Hurry disembarked from the steamship SS

Jervis Bay onto Australian soil at Fremantle and later, on the 29th September 1931, Eileen Nora Brooks set foot in Australia in Fremantle disembarking from the SS Largs Bay.[6] They made their way to Yelverton in Busselton, Sussex Land District, situated on the Margaret River and, typical of the lush Western Australia landscape, this is home to 140 different kinds of bird, ranging from the Pacific Black Duck to the Dusky Woodswallow.[7]

ABERDEEN AND COMMONWEALTH LINE S.S. "JERVIS BAY."
ONE CLASS SERVICE BETWEEN ENGLAND AND AUSTRALIA VIA SUEZ.

"LARGS BAY"

Photographs © Photo Archive

The Margaret River Region is an area of magnificent beauty on the South West Coast of the beautiful state of Western Australia, stretching from Busselton on the shores of Geographe Bay down to Augusta the most south-westerly point in Australia. [8]

Sydney Hurry in his 'best bib & tucker outside 53 St. John's Wood High Street

The WA Parks and Wildlife Service describes the forest region of Yelverton as, "Native forest containing a particularly diverse range of vegetation types and a high concentration of declared rare and priority flora species." [9]

In 1931, the world was still recovering from the disastrous economic effects of the First World War and the Great Worldwide Slump of 1929. The collapse of the Austrian Anstalt Bank had a devastating effect on the British trade along with the rest of the world. As the output of heavy industry fell by a third and profits plunged in nearly all sectors, the world started to feel the effects of the Great Depression, which followed the Wall Street crash in 1929.

Unemployment among the areas of heavy industry in the UK was as high as 70% and this tended to bring the mood of the nation down and caused resentment, dissent and despair.

Australia also felt the effects of the slump and suffered years of high unemployment, poverty, low profits, deflation, plunging incomes, and lost opportunities for economic growth and personal advancement during the Great Depression[10]. The National Archives of Australia, in their article "Immigration 1901–39: An Overview"; states, *"Immigration has been a vital feature of Australia's history and identity. The composition of the nation today includes not only its own indigenous peoples but also a wide variety of ethnic and cultural groups. Although Australia has always been multicultural, for at least a century and a half after European settlement, the*

British predominated. This was especially so in the period from Federation until World War II…"

There was though, a widespread concern about the slow rate of growth of the Australian population which had increased from 3¾ million in 1901 to only seven million in 1939. However, these low population numbers attracted immigrants to "…the land of opportunity…" and approximately 100,000 Europeans settled in Australia between the two World Wars; and during the 1930s, the balance between British and non-British immigrants was slowly becoming more equal…

Throughout the period from 1901–39, Australian immigration policy was governed by fixed notions of the preferred ethnic origins of prospective immigrants, the dictates of the labour market and the perceived need to settle people in rural areas rather than in the cities. To some, Australia could never have enough immigrants; to others, immigration was the principal cause of unemployment and social unrest."

"It is important to note that a large proportion of potential immigrants to Australia did not fit into either category of restricted immigrants or those who were actively encouraged. Australia allowed many thousands to come under the then current immigration policy but these immigrants did not receive any form of pecuniary assistance by governments or private organisations. They were generally ordinary working-class people who were migrating to better their lives and provide greater opportunities for their children."

Sydney and Eileen were two people who fitted into this category and they joined 268 other tourist class passengers on board their respective ships.

As discussed earlier in this chapter, Australia in 1931 was a colony of the British Empire and consequently under direct rule and the dispensing of justice through transportation from London.

Unlike Tasmania and New South Wales, Western Australia had never been a penal colony. Rather it was established in 1829 and was founded largely in response to what *An Economic History of WA since colonial settlement - WA Treasury* calls "enthusiastic" marketing by Captain James Stirling, a British naval officer and colonial administrator. He became the first Governor and Commander-in-Chief of the colony. [10] The move was a strategic one by the British as well, in order to prevent the

French from settling the non-annexed western third of the Australian continent.

Following two decades of unprecedented growth and prosperity, the Western Australian economy went through a period of severe hardship, as a result of a combination of both world and local events. Two world wars, an international depression and a major drought impacted the economy collectively, during a period when the State was attempting to readjust after the gold mining boom, which peaked in 1903.[11]

The Western Australia Treasury Report of the State finances in the years 1913 – 1946 states; "….the economy underwent significant structural change and economic growth was uneven at best. As the effects of the gold rush died down, mining's share of the economy declined and both the rural and manufacturing industries' shares increased…"

The prosperity of the agricultural industry changed throughout this period; following an expansion from 1903 to 1914, a severe drought and the start of the First World War hindered growth, with agricultural output of wheat falling by 80% in a single year. Only intervention in the form of subsidies by the government of the day and a 90% increase in the price of wheat between 1914 and 1920 managed to save the industry from total ruin.

The State's primary export commodity, wool production, expanded rapidly between 1926 and 1934, despite prices falling by 60% in 1930-31.

The War had had a disastrous effect on the numbers of mainly young men in the state and this shortage of ability and labour in agriculture threatened to shatter the already precarious state of the sheep and poultry farming industry.

What was needed was new blood and there was a ready market of recently unemployed young men and their families in Great Britain. As previously noted earlier in this chapter, the '....decision had already been taken by the Australian Government that Assisted Passage was not something that they favoured....' They reasoned that there could be no guarantees that immigrants would gravitate to, and eventually settle in, the areas and States that required them. The thinking was that, if families had already decided to emigrate and they had the requisite skills, why should their adopted country bear the cost of such an undertaking.

There was, however, a *'White Alien' Immigration Policy*[12], (the term white alien' was widely used in the period from 1901 to 1939 to describe non-British Europeans and was particularly directed towards Italians, Greeks, Yugoslavs and Poles). Regulations were adopted, which required all 'alien' migrants to possess £40 landing money (worth approximately £1900 in 2019), or hold landing permits issued as a result of their maintenance being guaranteed by relatives or friends in Australia or formal offers of employment .

This policy favoured Sydney and Eileen. They entered the State of Western Australia with little or no hindrance and once settled there, Eileen gave birth, first to John in 1931 and Josephine Edith on the 3rd August 1936.

Happy though they were in their lives as a sheep and poultry farmer and homemaker in Busselton, a disaster was about to beset them. A severe drought in 1935 through to 1939 devastated the woollen industry in Western Australia. In 1935, the rural areas of Western Australia supported 5½ million sheep and poultry but, during the next 5 years, 4 million sheep and poultry died in the drought. By 1946 and long after the drought had ended, sheep and poultry numbers were still only half the numbers recorded in 1935.[12]

It was the worst of times in Australia for the ordinary man and woman and particularly in the Western State. In the 1920s Australia collectively, (i.e. all of the individual States), had borrowed heavily abroad and met repayments through further short-term loans.[19] After the 1929 Wall Street stock market crash however, loans were recalled and cash flow diminished or dried up altogether, relating particularly to the governments, which had undertaken large capital works such as the wheat belt railway expansion in WA. In addition, the contraction in world trade during the depression led to commodity prices falling dramatically. Unemployment reached almost one third of the total workforce during the peak of the depression.

In 1937, the rumblings of war were echoing in Oceania, Asia and the Antipodes as the Japanese Empire attempted to dominate and occupy Asia and the Pacific. Very soon, over 100 million people from over 30 countries were in a state of war. It was the deadliest conflict in human history, remembered forever for the 75 million people who gave their lives.

The *Australian War Memorial*[19] recalls that; "On the 3rd of September 1939 Prime Minister Robert Gordon Menzies announced, on every national and commercial radio station in Australia, the beginning of Australia's involvement in the Second World War."

SS Moreton Bay

So, Sydney, Eileen, John and Josephine made their way to Fremantle and on Monday, 4 July 1938, they embarked the SS Moreton Bay and commenced the 65-day journey back to Southampton, arriving in the UK on Wednesday 7th September 1938.

All four of them are recorded next, as living in a leafy suburban street in Hendon in a 3 bedroomed semi-detached house and very close to the Hendon Airfield, as

John and Josephine outside the Post Office in Busselton

it was and also close to the Metropolitan Police Training School, known in 1938 as the Peel Centre. During the war, and for a time prior to the outbreak in 1939, it would have been quite a noisy and busy area with aeroplanes landing and taking off.

In May 1945 just prior to the end of the war, the records show Sydney and Eileen on the 'Civilian Residence Register' (*Author's note: as required under the National*

Registration Act 1939) in Potton, a village in Bedfordshire, near to Hitchin.

At the age of 16, Andy's mother Helen, who lived most of her early life in a convent orphanage in Dundee, decided to 'up sticks' and travel south to London to follow her dream of becoming a nun.

Andy's dad, John also aged 16 was now living with Mum and Dad, Sydney and Eileen, at Manor Park Road, Willesden and as we shall see later, coincidentally just 150 yards from the Convent of Jesus and Mary School in Crownhill Road.

Sadly, the house that they lived in is not there now and in its place is a shopping precinct.

---o0o--

Chapter 2

Root & Branch

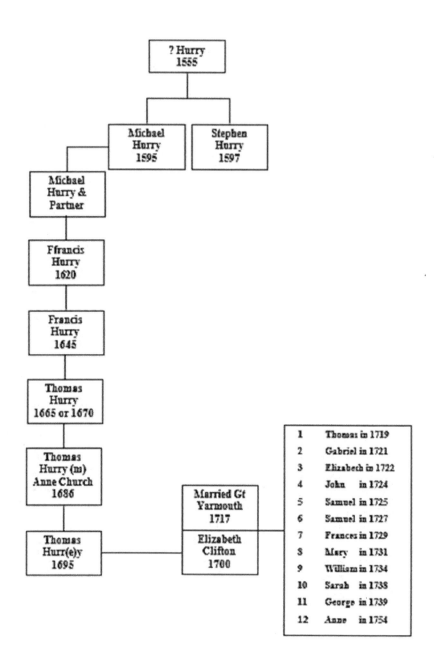

Chapter 2
Root and Branch

The earliest known recorded account of the name *Hurry* is in the 16th century, with an unknown Hurry born in 1555 in Norfolk. Two boys resulted from the unidentified partnership, Michael in 1595 and Stephen in 1597, both born in

Norfolk. Stephen was Michael's half-brother so, although the records cannot be located, there were at least two partners for the unnamed Hurry.

Michael and his unknown partner had a son, Ffrancis in 1620. (*The Ff at the beginning of the name is common in the Welsh language, with 'F' sounding as a soft 'V' and 'FF' a hard 'F' and is classed grammatically as a capital 'F'*[1])

Ffrancis and an unnamed partner had a son, Francis born in 1645. Francis and *his* unknown partner had a son Thomas, born in 1665 or 1670 (because two identical records record two different birthdates). He married Anne Church in Suffolk in 1686; they had a son, another Thomas born in 1695 and around this time, the entry spelt the surname, both with an 'e' and without an 'e'. Thomas, who was born in Great Yarmouth, married Elizabeth

Clifton in 1717. She was born in 1700 also in Great Yarmouth and they had eleven children

1. Thomas in 1719   *5*. Samuel in 1725 or 1727

2. Gabriel *in* 1721   *6*. Frances in 1729   *9*. Sarah in 1738

3.Elizabeth in 1722   *7*. Mary in 1731   *10*. George in 1739

4. John In 1724   *8*. William in 1734   *11*. Anne in 1754

Entries in the *London Directory of 1791*[2] list Samuel, William and Thomas as Merchants and it is recorded that they owned a vast whale fishing fleet of fifteen ships operating in the South Sea Whale Fishery.

THE

LONDON DIRECTORY

For the YEAR 1791;

CONTAINING

AN ALPHABETICAL ARRANGEMENT

OF THE

NAMES and Residences of the MERCHANTS, MA-
NUFACTURERS and PRINCIPAL TRADERS in the
METROPOLIS and its Environs, with the Number
affixed to each House;

ALSO

SEPARATE LISTS OF THE LORD MAYOR AND
COURT OF ALDERMEN,

COMMISSIONERS OF CUSTOMS. EXCISE AND STAMPS;

DIRECTORS OF THE BANK, SOUTH-SEA, EAST-
INDIA AND RUSSIA COMPANIES;

ROYAL EXCHANGE, LONDON ASSURANCE, SUN, UNION,
HAND IN HAND, PHOENIX AND WESTMINSTER
FIRE OFFICES;

TO WHICH ARE ADDED,

The FIRMS of the different BANKING HOUSES
And a particular Account of the PUBLIC FUNDS.

PRINTED FOR W. LOWNDES, No. 77, FLEET-STREET.

They commissioned the building of five ships in Britain, (the most likely place being North Shields), five in France and at least one each in Spain, Bermuda and the East Indies.

Jane M. Clayton and Charles A. Clayton in their excellent reference book, '*Ship owners investing in the South Sea Whale Fishery from Britain: 1775-1815*[3]', write that the Hurry family had strong links to Great Yarmouth, Liverpool, Australia and America; and, as we shall see later in the book, they also had a significant participation in the American War of Independence. Although it is not noted in the Clayton's book, the Hurry family also had strong links to another port town in the North East, namely North Shields. When they sent their ship the *Ocean* to Australia in 1803, other fleet operators considered them to be 'newly operating south fishers'[3].

Their father Captain Thomas Hurry, born in 1696, was a Master Mariner from Great Yarmouth, who moved to Rotherhithe, which, in the eighteenth century was an important port in the City of London. The Norfolk Chronicle of 19th August 1780[4] recorded his death thus...

Last week died in London, in the 86th year of his age, Mr Thomas HURRY, of Yarmouth.

There are conflicting accounts as to where he passed away. The record showed that he died at the Adelphi Hotel, Villiers Street, just off the Strand, in what was then the County of Middlesex; however, there is another report of him passing away in Greenwich.

It is possible that he passed away in the hotel and his body transported by boat to Greenwich. Suffice to say, he passed away near the River Thames and the sea that he was wedded to and on which he had spent most of his adult working life.

Detail of the River Thames with St. Paul's Cathedral on Lord Mayors Day by Canaletto
Print reproduced courtesy ©National Portrait Gallery

The atmospheric painting; 'View of St Paul's from the Thames', by Canaletto and painted in or around 1746, illustrates quite succinctly the scarcity of bridges over the Thames in the eighteenth century. The painting also shows how busy the river was, with the many, numerous sailing ships and small craft wending their way up, down and across the Thames from the North embankment to the South embankment. Thomas Hurry junior, born in 1719, assumed control of his father's fleet of three ships, The Brunswick, The Ocean and The York after his father passed away.

A fine example of a 'copper-bottomed' trading ship. Reproduced courtesy of John P Birchill

Mr Thomas Hurry, the Brunswick 483 tons
the Ocean 481 tons
York 397 tons
for four voyages to Bengal, at £1.33 per ton in war and £.20 in peace and the furplus tonnage half freight, in each cafe of which he ftates they can carry a confiderable, fo as to reduce the freight very materially

In the publication –

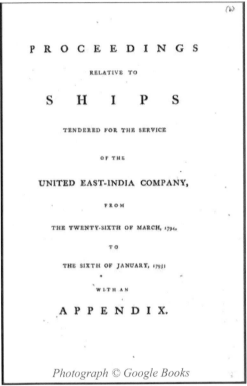

PROCEEDINGS

RELATIVE TO

SHIPS

TENDERED FOR THE SERVICE

OF THE

UNITED EAST-INDIA COMPANY,

FROM

THE TWENTY-SIXTH OF MARCH, 1794,

TO

THE SIXTH OF JANUARY, 1795;

WITH AN

APPENDIX.

Photograph © Google Books

It was ordered, that the following perfons be defired to fend in frefh tenders of fhips on Tuefday next, before 11 o'clock, ftating terms of freight and conforming to the terms above-mentioned in every particular, viz

 Meffrs. St Barbe, Green and
 Bignell
 Mr. William Chriftopher
 Ralph Keddey
 Henry Bonham
 Peter Everitt Meftaer
 John Woolmore
 William Hamilton
 Thos. Hurry.

Following the announcement that shipping companies were invited to submit requests of interest in tendering for future work with the United East India Company, the following notice observes that Thomas was indeed successful in his submission.

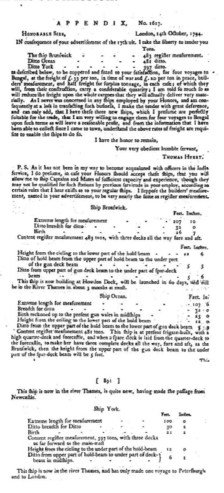

The records show that Thomas tendered for; "…. four Voyages to Bengal…" Thomas passed away in 1801 in Great Yarmouth as the following from the Clayton's book shows.

…. occupation Great Yarmouth, Norfolk. Merchant and Ship Owner, and senior partner in the agency house for many years conducted under the style of Messrs Thomas Hurry and Co.

Thomas Hurry (b.dnic - d.dnic). There are several Thomas Hurrys in the family, all of whom have links with shipbuilding and maritime professions, either in Great Yarmouth or London. Capt. Thomas Hurry (b.1696 - d.1780) moved from Yarmouth to Rotherhithe and he had a son, also Thomas who died in 1801. Samuel, William and Thomas, three brothers, and Edward are listed as

Thomas' brother Samuel, born on Christmas Day in 1727 in [Great] Yarmouth, was also a shipping merchant with a vast fleet of at least a dozen ships.

In the year 1754, at the age of 27, he is living in Yarmouth. His grandfather, Thomas Hurrey (sic) (1665-1750) is recorded as being a; 'Hemp and Iron Merchant, a shipping agent, a Vice Consul to Prussia (unconfirmed) and working and living in 133 King Street, Great Yarmouth. It appears that at one time the whole family was living in the property.

133 King Street is a Grade II listed building, listed on the 'Listed Buildings website'[5] thus –

"Late C17 house with attached warehouse to rear remodelled late C18. Converted to shop with accommodation c1885, altered late C20. C18 facade. Red brick with burnt headers. Roof of Black-glazed pantiles"

133 King Street in c1865

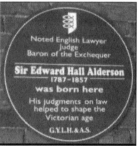

Blue plaque outside 133

The relationship between the influential & important Hall, Hurry & Alderson families.

Samuel Hurry married Isabelle Hall on the 27th June 1750 in Yarmouth. They had two children, Elizabeth, born on the 10th May 1751 and Samuel junior born on January the 20th 1754.

On the 16th November 1784, Elizabeth married Robert Alderson, son of the Reverend James Alderson, born in 1714 in Westmorland in the Lake District.

Robert's parents were James Alderson and Isabel Weatherill. It is self-evident that the Hall, Hurry and Alderson families were prosperous, successful and very wealthy.

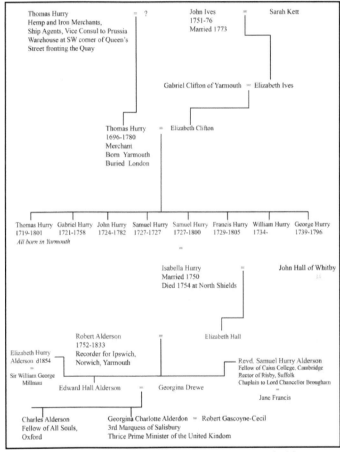

Family tree showing the link between the Hurry and Alderson families in Gt Yarmouth, reproduced courtesy of Paul P Davies

The following is a publication of 1810 -

A LIST OF THE DIVINITY STUDENTS EDUCATED AT DR. ROTHERAM'S ACADEMY, KENDAL; WITH THE PLACES WHERE THEY AFTERWARDS SETTLED, AND SHORT MEMOIRS OF SOME INDIVIDUALS. 1733.

1 James Alderson

This gentleman settled at Lowestoffe (sic), (probably succeeding Mr. Say.) He died in 1761, leaving a widow, Mrs. Judith Alderson, who is still alive, standing first upon the list of that excellent institution, (established in 1733,) the Society established in London for the Relief of the Necessitous Widows and Children of Protestant Dissenting Ministers deceased.

By great exertions, she [has been] enabled to bring up a large family, most of whom have made a considerable figure in the world.

1. Her eldest son, James Alderson, M.D. was long an eminent surgeon, and is now a physician, in Norwich. His daughter is the celebrated Quaker Amelia Alderson, later Amelia Opie, who became famous as a writer and proponent of emancipation. [Author's note: wife of the eminent painter John Opie.]

2.   Thomas resided long in the West Indies, and having made a handsome fortune, settled at Durham, where he died a few years ago.

3.   Robert, was educated at Warrington, for the ministry among Protestant Dissenters, and was, for several years, one of the ministers at the Octagon Chapel, in Norwich. About 1787, he married Elizabeth, daughter of William Hurry, **[Author's note; please note the correction in the succeeding letter.***) Esq. of Yarmouth and, not long after, quitted the ministry and embraced the profession of the law. He is now recorder of Ipswich and steward of Norwich. His wife's uncle, Edward Hall, Esq. of Whitley, Northumberland, published from his manuscripts, "Specimens of Sermons and Prayers, by a late Divine; printed for Johnson, 1788." If his eldest son, Edward Hall Alderson, was senior wrangler and medallist at Cambridge last year; his second son, third wrangler this year; his daughter lately married the son of Sir Francis Milman, Bart (President of the Royal College of Physicians of London).*

4.   *John is an eminent physician at Hull, and an active promoter of agricultural improvements, as well as of general science and literature.*

5.   *A daughter of Mrs. Alderson's married a Mr. Woodhouse, of Norwich, and had four sons: Olyett, a counsellor at Bombay; Robert, the very eminent professor of mathematics at Cambridge; James, a surgeon in the army; and Richard, a merchant in Hull.*

A letter in The Monthly Repository of Theology and General Literature, Volume 5, published on August the 2nd 1810 corrects the name of the husband of Elizabeth and verifies the pedigree as detailed in this book.

Errors in the Account of the Alderson Family.

To the Editor of the Monthly Repository. Temple, London, Aug. 2, 1810.

SIR,

*I feel much indebted to you for the very interesting account of the students educated under Dr. Rotherham; it is in many respects gratifying, but in some humiliating to a Nonconformist (**author's note: a Protestant who did not*** *"conform" to the governance and usages of the established Church of England)... But let that pass. My object in taking up my pen is solely to correct an error or two, into which you have fallen, in your memoirs of James Alderson.*

*Mr. Robert Alderson, the quondam (**author's note: means erstwhile**) minister, married the daughter of Mr. Samuel Hurry, not of Mr. William Hurry. His children, by that marriage, inherit the ample fortune of their maternal grandfather, in consequence of the death of his only son, Mr. Samuel Hurry, jun. Mr. W. Hurry, who died a short time ago, was the brother of Mr. Samuel Hurry, and the father of the late Mr. Edmund Hurry, of Mr. Ives Hurry, of Mrs. Maurice, of Normanston, of Mrs. George Morgan, &c. &c.*

You are surely mistaken, too, in saying that the venerable Mrs. Alderson stands "first upon the list of the Society for the Relief of the necessitous Widows and Children of Protestant Dissenting

Ministers deceased." Your own account of her opulent family ("one of whom died a few years ago leaving a *handsome fortune,") might of itself have suggested to you, that you were in an error. If I had possessed the list referred to, I doubt not but I could do away your misrepresentation, which, however, I impute to inadvertence only. You certainly are not aware that no widow can receive relief from the fund you mention, without declaring that she has not an income exceeding twenty-five pounds per annum! I can only account for your blunder, in describing Mrs. Alderson as dependant (sic) upon eleemosynary* charity, by supposing that, in the haste of preparing your work for the press, your eye fell upon the wrong list, in the annual statement of the Widow's Fund Society; and that you extracted the name of Alderson, not from the list of widows receiving assistance, but from that of subscribers, where it is very probable the name may be found more than once.*

It is possible, indeed, that in one of the statements of the Widow's Fund, years back, when the Alderson family were just rising into prosperity, the case may have been as you say; and, you may have consulted one of these obsolete publications; or, by a ridiculous blunder, the name may

*have been yearly reprinted. At any rate the mistake should
be rectified.*

*I am not acquainted with any of the members of this
numerous and prosperous family, but I wish to see justice
done to all persons, for, I am, by principle and long
profession, A NonCon.*

* Definition of Eleemosynary by Merriam-Webster.
The good people of early England had mercy on
themselves when it came to spelling and shortened the
root of "eleemosynary," the Latin eleemosyna, to
"ælmes," which they used as their word for "charity."
(You may be more familiar with "alms," an "ælmes"
derivative that came to denote food or money given to the
poor as in alms-houses.)

---o0o---

Chapter 3

Downing Street

Chapter 3

Downing Street

Notwithstanding the Hurrys' influence in orchestrating change in British politics, they also had a significant part to play in the American War of Independence, which was creating turmoil in the United Kingdom.

James E Bradley, in his excellent book, ***Popular Politics and the American Revolution in England***[1], writes about the political atmosphere around the English Army in the war of American Independence. *"Popular agitation concerning America was as widespread in the English provinces as other popular protests in the 1770s and 1780s. The petitions also penetrated deeply into the populace; frequently more than half of those who petitioned, were not qualified to vote in parliamentary elections.*

Author's note: *In an age of aristocracy, where the views and opinions of the people were often viewed with disdain, the Hurry family would be instrumental in enabling **The Representation of the People Act 1832** (also known as the **1832 Reform Act, Great Reform Act or First Reform Act.** (albeit 2 generations hence)*

GREAT YARMOUTH

Great Yarmouth was a medium-sized borough with a freeman electorate, and although there were some 800 voters, the corporation played an important part in borough politics. The corporation in turn was influenced by the Townshend and Walpole families who dominated borough politics from 1722 to 1784. Frequent political contests illustrate the existence of a viable opposition element that, though active, was kept under control through the port's heavy dependence on patronage. The corporation systematically excluded those whose politics ran counter to the government. Opposition to the corporation party in the second half of the century was organized by the Nonconformists.[20]

The attempt to take the control of patronage from the Townshend-Walpole monopoly and the corporation began in 1768 and extended through 1784. The opposition faction was organized by ten of the town's leading Dissenters, headed by the prominent Hurry family. Thomas Hurry and his sons were hemp and iron merchants with numerous ships and extensive warehouses in Queen Street.[21] A small coterie of disaffected corporation members constituted the Anglican side of the faction. In 1769 this group presented a remonstrance to the sitting members of Parliament that attacked John Ramey, the Townshend-Walpole agent, for neglecting their own special interests. The opposition, deriving nearly half of its force from the Dissenters, was threatening enough to cause Ramey's resignation, but little else was accomplished.[22] In the general election of 1774, the opposition put forth Sir Charles Saunders, a friend and supporter of Rockingham, and William Beckford, son of the well-known London radical. At a by-election in 1777 they backed Beckford again, but in both elections they made a poor showing at the polls.[23] In 1780 the independents signed a petition for economic reform, and in 1782 and 1783 attempts were made to change the prevailing channels of patronage by means of further appeals for parliamentary reform.[24] In their last attempt, the Yarmouth independents turned to the Reverend George Walker, the Presbyterian minister, as their spokesman. In his various approaches to Lord Shelburne, Walker was also unsuccessful, but when Pitt's government pronounced against the sitting members at the general election of 1784, the opposition won both parliamentary seats. At this point, the independents themselves became the main channel of government patronage to local placemen.

Although the Dissenting interest at Great Yarmouth was not large, all four of the major denominations were represented. The Goal Street Presbyterian Chapel was the most prominent in size and influence, and it was the chosen home of the Hurry family. There was a Congregational chapel of unknown size, and in the course of the eighteenth century a second Baptist meeting was added to the existing one. A small Quaker assembly rounded out the full complement of Dissenting options, but none of the meetings put forward a single prominent clerical leader during the years of the American crisis.[25] Of the four known Dissenting ministers who might have supported conciliation in 1775, only one in fact did.[26]

Popular Politics and the American Revolution in England

What was lacking in the clergy, however, was supplied by the laity. The Hurry family had taken the initiative against the local monopoly in the 1760s, and they, with a number of their brethren, provided constant leadership for opposition politics. The Presbyterian baptismal register graphically illustrates the family's connection to the independent faction. In 1762 William Hurry named his first son Edmund Cobb. Cobb's namesake was, like Hurry himself, a leading Yarmouth independent. In 1777, when the opposition party put up William Beckford against the government interest for the second time, Hurry named his fourth son Beckford, after William Beckford, thereby symbolizing the family's longstanding attachment to radical causes.[27] Five of the six Hurrys who voted in this election voted for Beckford.[28] After the American crisis the family continued to take politics seriously. In the late 1780s, Thomas and Thomas Hurry, Jr., Samuel and Samuel Hurry, Jr., George and William Hurry all purchased freeholds at Norwich for the purpose of voting in Norwich elections, and in the contest of 1786 they all voted for the opposition candidate.[29]

The leaders of the independent party were also prominent in the local resistance to the government's American policy.[30] The agitation regarding America began on 26 September 1775 when the mayor called the corporation together for the purpose of addressing the Crown in favor of coercive measures. Four days later a second coercive address was circulated among the population and it ultimately gained 227 signatures. Among the signers was John Ramey, the former agent of the Townshend-Walpole interest—who was by this date placated by a government pension—and his successor as government agent, William Fisher. Both addresses supporting coercion were presented by the faithful supporter of North and sitting member of Yarmouth, Charles Townshend of Honingham. It was not until six weeks later that a conciliatory petition reached London. It had collected 347 signatures. While only one of the Presbyterian ministers signed this petition, the leadership of the Dissenting laity is likely in that seven of the first ten signatures were Presbyterian and five members of the Hurry family also signed the document.[31] The American crisis had provided yet another occasion for the local opposition faction to express its disaffection toward the government, but it can be argued that the plea for peace illustrated something more exalted than pique over their exclusion from political perquisites.

The Nonconformists[2] were members of several Protestant groups outside of the Church of England. They included in their ranks the Old Dissenters, denominations that went back to the seventeenth century. The largest body then had been the Presbyterians, who believed that there should be no bishops since all ministers were equal (i.e. a "ministry of all believers"). In the eighteenth century, the Old Dissenters normally supported the Whig politicians who promised the greatest degree of civil and religious liberty, though the Wesleyans, following their founder John Wesley, endorsed the existing authorities in church and state. At the time of the American Revolution, for example, many Dissenting ministers spoke out for the colonists... With the help of liberal Whig peers, repeal came in 1828. Dissenters, many of whom retained deep suspicions of Papal ambitions, were divided over Roman Catholic emancipation in the following year, but nearly all welcomed the Great Reform Act of 1832. The Municipal Corporations Act of 1835, by opening councils to election by ratepayers, enabled many Dissenters to enter local government. They were therefore a growing political force by the 1830s, firmly aligned with the progressive side in national affairs.

In that decade, the Non-conformists, as they were just beginning to be called, had a number of grievances that they wanted to have redressed by the reformed Parliament. Births in their families went unrecorded unless their infants were baptised in the Church of England; legal marriages could be celebrated only in the Church of England, with Quakers and Jews being the sole exceptions; burials in parish churchyards had to follow the Book of Common Prayer read by the parish clergyman;

only Anglicans were allowed to enter the University of Oxford and to graduate from the University of Cambridge; and in each parish Dissenters were liable to pay the rate for the upkeep of the parish church. Resentment against these inequalities boiled over in 1833-34 in an agitation for their removal. The Whig government tried unsuccessfully to open the universities to Dissenters and, by introducing civil registration of births and permission for Dissenters to use their own buildings for marriage, dealt with two of the grievances, but the others continued to fester, yoking Nonconformists firmly to the Liberal Party that alone would help them. Compulsory church rates were abolished by Gladstone in 1868, most university tests ended in 1871 and burials were allowed with Non-conformist rites from 1880.

So, it appears that the Hurry family felt disenfranchised from the political elite and their views and opinions on the colonies were not being heard. The Hurrys' however, were slowly becoming a powerful voice in Norfolk, Suffolk and the North East of England. Towards the end of the 18th century their influence was being recognised and they were beginning to move in more exclusive circles. Elizabeth, born in 1791 in Yarmouth was the daughter of William Hurry and Elizabeth Dann. By the age of 18, she had met and married the second Baronet Sir William George Milman. Sir William was governor of the Old Bailey and his principal family seat was at The Grove, Pinner.

This is his entry in the Oxford University alumni record

Alumni Oxoniensis (1715-1886) volume 3. djvu/177

Milman, Robert, as. William George, of Easton-in-Gordano, Somerset, baronet. Exeter Coll., matric 9 May, 1833, aged 17; scholar 1834-8, B.A. 1838, M.A. 1867, created D.D. 30 Jan., 1867, bishop of Calcutta, 1867-76, vicar of Chaddleworth 184051, of Lamborne, Bucks, 1851-62, and of Great Marlow, Bucks, 1862-7, died 15 March, 1876. See Foster's Baronetage & Coll. Re* 15a.

Lady Elizabeth (as she was known formally) and Sir William retired to Pinner Grove, (the family seat for three generations until 1860) where they resided with the other members of the family and the household staff–

William Geo Milman	*60*	*Harry Milman*	*52*
Elizabeth Harry Milman	*59*	*Footman Henry Bradley*	*35*
Matilda F Milman	*31*	*Coachman James Whistler*	*17*
Frances Tho Milman	*3*	*Page Mary Ann Reed*	*33*

Hugh Nick Milman	5	Cook Jane Fletchcock	27
William G Milman	2	Ladies Maid Mary Tinant	26
Katherine Milman	6	House Maid Arley Stillwell	20
Isabella Milman	4	Milk Maid Hannah Huzzell	19
Kitchen Maid Susan Skimmer	21	Phillip R Alderson Attorney	21

Meanwhile, on another branch of the family tree, Samuel Hurry, *someone who has already been discussed in this book*, married Isabella Hall. They had a daughter Elizabeth, born in 1751 in 133 King Street, Yarmouth. In 1784, she married Robert Alderson, Recorder for Ipswich, Norwich and Yarmouth. He became a Baron of the Court of Exchequer[3] in 1834. They had a son, Edward Hall Alderson, born, also at 133 King Street, in 1787. He was to become Baron Edward Hall Alderson. Elizabeth died in 1791 and in 1852; Robert married again, this time to Henrietta Maria Mannock, born in Cromer.

In 2006, the Octagon Chapel in Colegate, Norwich celebrated its 250th anniversary and to honour this event, the Eastern Daily Press published this anecdote of Baron Robert Alderson.

".... One of my favourites is the Rev. Robert Alderson, co-pastor of the Octagon from 1776-1786, when the chapel was in its heyday as one of the chief intellectual centres of England, renowned for the learning, scholarship, brilliance and wit of those who worshipped there.

Robert Alderson was the son of the Rev. James Alderson, a minister at Lowestoft, and the younger brother of Dr James Alderson, the distinguished physician, (father of Amelia Opie), whose house - a little further along the street - faced the parish church of St George Colegate. After concluding that he preferred law to gospel, the Rev.

'Pistols at Dawn' by Stephen Liddell

Robert Alderson resigned and exchanged the pulpit for the bar. He prospered in his new career, (the two being - in some respects - not dissimilar: both concerned with advocacy, and both usefully embellished with a modicum of acting ability!) On August 17 1802, a duel was fought on Mousehold Heath by Robert Alderson and a Mr. Grigby, who felt he had been unfairly treated in cross examination by Mr. Alderson at the Suffolk Assizes. Grigby refused to accept his explanation and sent him a challenge. Mr. Alderson was attended to the field by Mr. Mackintosh, and Mr. Grigby by Mr. Turner.

Two shots were exchanged, with no effect other than that of Mr. Grigby's first ball passing through the skirts of Mr. Alderson's coat. A *'...cordial reconciliation was afterwards realised...'*!

Robert Alderson succeeded Charles Harvey as Recorder of Norwich, and lived long enough to see his son, Edward Hall Alderson, appointed a Judge in the Court of Common Pleas. (He became a Baron of the Court of Exchequer in 1834.)

On 25th October 1823, Edward Hall Alderson married Georgina Catherine Drewe in Great Yarmouth. She was born in 1799 in Broadhembury, Devon to Edward Drewe and Caroline Allen.

They had ten children who were all successful in their individual lives, but notable were Charles Henry born in 1831, who became a fellow of All Souls, Oxford and

Georgina Caroline born in 1826, who married Robert Arthur Talbot Gascoyne-Cecil, the Third Marquess of Salisbury in 1857. The Third Marquess of Salisbury was the last Prime Minister to run Britain from the House of Lords between June 1885 and his retirement in 1902.

"Civilised, humorous, cynical and likeable, the Victorian Titan", as his biographer Andrew Roberts calls him, *"was born Robert Arthur Talbot Gascoyne-Cecil in 1830 at Hatfield House, his family's stately home in Hertfordshire. He was MP for Stamford in his twenties and thirties as Lord Robert Cecil (pronounced 'Sissle' by those familiar to him), succeeded as Marquess in 1868 and was foreign secretary under Disraeli in 1878-80".*

*"Lord Robert Cecil was born at Hatfield House, the second son of James Gascoyne-Cecil, 2nd Marquess of Salisbury and Frances Mary Gascoyne. He was a patrilineal **(Editor's note: relating to descent through the male line)** descendant of Lord Burghley and the first Earl of Salisbury, who were chief ministers of Elizabeth I **(1533-1603)**. The family owned vast rural estates in Hertfordshire and Dorset. This wealth increased sharply in 1821, when he married the rich heiress of a merchant*

prince who had bought up large estates in Essex and Lancashire"[2]

---oOo---

Amelia Alderson Opie

John Opie self portrait

Detail from the portrait of Robert Alderson,
reproduced courtesy © National Portrait Gallery

We now have a determined lineage of the Hurry family, direct from the First Earl of Salisbury, one of Queen Elizabeth 1st ministers and through their pedigree to a connection to 10, Downing Street and a British Prime Minister…

Lord & Lady Cecil Robert Gascoyne Cecil, 3rd Marquess of Salisbury

Marquess of Salisbury Coat of Arms

A young Andy in conversation with dad, John in his cricket whites.

Andy, aged 3 with his first cricket bat

Andy and Peter at Christmas

Peter and Andy

Peter, Mum, Dad and Andy

Andy and Mum Helen Margaret

Chapter 4

A Tale of Two Brothers

Chapter 4

A Tale of Two Brothers

Sir Trevor Brooking, the *'polite and patient man[1]'* of football, wrote in his 18-chapter book, My Life in Football[2]. *"...as a youngster, growing up in Barking, I would spend hours kicking a tennis ball against a wall, trapping and controlling it with my weaker left foot, until I could control it as well as I did with my right foot.*

People tell me they were surprised I wasn't left-footed when I played football as I could trap, control, pass and shoot the ball as well with my right foot as with my left foot".

At the age of seven, Lewis Hamilton made his first appearance on TV, on Blue Peter[3], presenter John Leslie knelt to speak to the boy, who stood glassy-eyed beside a miniature racetrack; he introduced a name that has since become synonymous with Grand Prix racing. "Lewis Hamilton is only seven years old..." enthused Leslie, glancing across at the child. Lewis didn't return the look. His focus was elsewhere. The boy who made his TV debut back in 1992 was not yet old enough to race on a circuit. Instead, Lewis was piloting a radio-controlled car, a hobby for which he'd shown prodigious talent.

Justin Langer, in his book, 'Seeing the Sunrise'[4], recalls;
"*I am told, as a young boy, I would inform anyone who would listen that I would play cricket for Australia. Every summer I would run around the backyard with my brothers, pretending to be one of my cricket heroes. If these champions had the ability to play fantastic shots or bowl like the wind, why couldn't I?*"

He continues; "*Steve Waugh often told me how he would visualise a score on the scoreboard before a Test had even started. It was as though he had completed his innings before he went out to bat. Justin Hogan, a friend of mine, who is a sports psychologist, once described it this way; "....the most powerful form of dreaming or visualising is not as if you are watching a video of yourself but actually being intimately a part of the image, by feeling all the mental and physical experiences associated with peak performance*". It would be churlish and frankly wrong, to assume that only men can do this. Compare the performances of top female athletes such as Jessica Ennis-Hill, Paula Radcliffe, the Williams sisters, Tanni Grey-Thompson and Anya Shrubsole, amongst many others. Whether as part of a team or as an individual, the aforementioned all excel(led) in their chosen sports through total dedication and with the mind-set, even at a young age, to achieve and ultimately succeed.

There are other numerous rôle models I could have used, who would have illustrated the point effectively but for the purposes of exemplifying hard work, dedication, true grit, talent, ambition, a desire to succeed and to try to be better than your peers, the illustrations are apposite and quintessential. Andy can stand shoulder to shoulder alongside these and any other sportsman and woman as a true equal; he has the dedication, the drive and the requisite skills.

From the age of four, Andy would go with his father, John, to cricket or football *every weekend.* He would sit in the back seat of John's White Ford Capri, very often with other cricketers or footballers, who would sit in the front seat, to matches. He sat quietly, just listening intently to the conversations and becoming immersed in his own imagination, hitting a six over the pavilion at Lord's, bowling one of his right-arm deliveries and taking the prize scalp of Kim Hughes, the Australian Captain or scoring a goal from the halfway line, a feat which he accomplished on at least one occasion!

During the summer holidays, Andy and his brother Peter would wolf down their breakfast cereal, put on their plimsolls or football boots and meet up with other friends. They would stay out all day, in either the back garden, the park or the cricket ground at Delwood Avenue, the venue for Test matches or Cup finals. It was common for them to stay out all day until it went dark but on occasions they would come back home, coming in for the occasional drink to slake their parched throats with lashings of cold cordial or water. The atmosphere around the table at mealtimes would have been something to behold.

Such was the energy to play sports that, at times, the brothers would play

'proper' test matches, which lasted for five days; there were, however, a few more than twenty wickets taken!

Andy and Peter were close as children and both will admit readily that each was an inspiration to the other. This sentiment is an indication of the degree of trust and love between the brothers. This bond was formed and nurtured by the love shown by their mother, Helen and father John. Andy has the fondest memories growing up and from his earliest recollection it is telling that his memories comprise many family holidays. One took place in

Norfolk and Suffolk, staying in hotels on the East Coast. Another was a two-week holiday in the Highlands of Scotland where Peter and Andy explored castles, took hill walks, and adored the thrill of cooking, eating and sleeping in a VW Campervan, borrowed by their father for the trip. Both brothers admit readily that they were phenomenal adventures.

Andy's eyes light up when he talks about his formative years. He had a loving mother, who worked tirelessly, and a doting father who inspired his passion for all sports. After football on a Saturday, they would throw their dirty clothes by the back door and, as children do, just expect Mum to wash them and for them to be clean next time they wanted them.

Andy continues; "Then we would jump straight in the bath. As soon as the bath was over, on Saturday afternoons, there'd be the wrestling on ITV and me and Pete used to watch the wrestling; Giant Haystacks, Big Daddy and the others and then we would strip down to our pants and wrestle, slamming each other into the front room carpet and forcing a submission".

All through his life, Andy's father had been a keen footballer and one of the teams he played for was Felixstowe Juniors. Andy stresses the fact that although this team was a called Felixstowe Juniors, his dad was in his fifties, playing alongside Andy's peers in their early twenties and Pete was a teenager! He was the Grandad of the team but everyone loved playing alongside him. It was fair to say, even though in his fifties, he was the fittest player in the team.

As boys, Andy and Pete had the measure and mutual respect of each other at a young age and I expect that just a look from either of them at a potential aggressor would be sufficient for the antagonist to back away.

One of Peter's recollections involves a snooker table. "I remember Andy getting a 4ft x 3ft Chad Valley snooker table. We were playing but we started to argue and the next thing it broke in one corner. From then, as you hit the balls, they all rolled down into one corner. Considering this was a new toy Andy was not angry about it being broken and he was more concerned that I was upset about it. This is a typical Andy virtue - thinking of others before himself.

The first time you meet Andy, you are struck by the way he greets you. A penetrating look, a slight upward curvature of the mouth, suggesting a hint of humour; a walnut-brown, chiselled, handsome face and a five-foot-ten-inch muscular frame. A firm handshake and suddenly

you are the most important person in the room. Never mind that you are talking to a man who has achieved so much. To this unassuming man, you are a key figure.

What Andy expects, and Peter does too, is honesty, trustworthiness and integrity. Very few people are able to carry this persona because it's not contrived, not manufactured. This elusive presence of personality, which in some may be clichéd - but in those who can achieve it, is charisma.

The corner house in Felixstowe had a large garden, which wrapped around it, and was spacious enough to allow the boys to have a long run up when bowling in one of their many countless games of cricket, sometimes with their mother acting as a bowler and erstwhile superb fielder.

Peter was a left arm bowler but he would bat right-handed. "Dad taught me so much about how to play cricket, although it came more naturally to Andrew";

Peter reminisces. "Dad was captain of both Bury St. Edmunds and Felixstowe Cricket Clubs and at every opportunity, at weekends and during the holidays; we'd be down at the club in the nets. Andy was a much more gifted cricketer than I was and I can see him now bowling ball after ball at a single stump in the nets. He was so dedicated."

"Cricket was always a family affair", Peter continues; "Mum would make the sandwiches and serve tea in the pavilion at lunch and tea breaks. Dad would stay after the match and run the bar or head off into town for a curry with the team". He was fully involved in the club, helping to maintain the square and outfield. Andy recalls; "The club was a big part of his life; it gave him real purpose and a sense of belonging".

Andy was born in Bushey in 1964 and Peter in 1968 after the family moved to a large detached house in Horringer Road, Bury St. Edmunds. John was a successful accountant and moving to Bury St Edmunds opened up more opportunities for him and his family. The address in Bury St. Edmunds may have been chosen due to its close proximity to the Cricket Ground, as it was only a short 5-minute drive away from the house on Nowton Road, in the Victory Sports Ground.

The Victory Sports Ground was created to commemorate the employees of Greene King who took part in World War I, many of whom passed away in the conflict, but it was Edward Lake who was working at Greene King in Bury St. Edmunds who came up with the idea to have a permanent memorial.

Edward, who was Managing Director of the company, persuaded the board of Greene King to purchase 26 acres of land and open a sports ground to commemorate the return of most of the brewery's workforce from the war. Edward and his wife Blanche had six sons (and six daughters) and all went to war during the Great War.

In 1975, Bury St. Edmunds Borough Council purchased the ground and operated it as a community facility. The quality of the ground, however, began to worsen and the cost implications to the Borough Council became significant; in fact, the cost to the council was in the region of £150,000 per year due, in most part, to having to employ two full-time grounds staff and the considerable council management costs.

Sadly, the quality of the ground deteriorated to such an extent that Suffolk stopped playing its Minor Counties matches there. After discussions with the club, a forward-thinking group of people formed a `not for profit` organisation, to take on the running and maintenance of the ground under a lease granted in 1995.

The ground improved steadily, became once again, one of the best sports grounds in East Anglia, and is now owned by The Victory Sports Community Interest Company, who purchased the ground from Bury St. Edmunds Borough Council on January 1st 2013. It has charitable status and has been made available for use by the local community.[4]

The first car both brothers remember their father owning was a white J registration Mark 1 Ford Capri which, when new would have cost around £900.[6]

Andy recalls it was beautiful, slick and fast. Andy's first car was also a Ford Capri Mark 1 and, according to Peter, a blue K-registration, which cost about £200. The lights only worked when they felt like it and often would randomly go off whilst driving. The car battery often went flat and this made him late for work but it was Andy's first car and he loved it. Peter's first car was a customised K-registration 850cc Mini, with bucket seats and wide wheels. Pete would drive to and from Suffolk to Taunton where he was based as a Royal Marine, a 520-mile round trip on a weekly basis.

Performance cars did and still do play a big part in Andy's life; they may have all seen better days and the memory of them faded but the influence his father had on him remains to this day.

In 1972 or 1973 the family moved from Bury St. Edmunds to Felixstowe and as well as playing cricket, Peter says; "We were fortunate to grow up in a seaside town so most of the summer holidays were spent down at the beach with

Ford Capri Mark 1

our Mum and on occasions Dad would come down in his lunch break for a swim and then head back to the office". Peter and Andy both have cherished memories of growing up with devoted parents, with Peter saying; "Mum was truly devoted to the family and was the backbone of the family and a constant in our lives. With the family enjoying a full schedule of school, church, football, cricket, running, youth club, Cubs, Scouts and later on Andy in the Air Cadets and myself joining the Sea Cadets, Mum was kept busy, but also left in the house on her own as we all amused ourselves indulging in our various activities. She also worked hard as a home help for the local council and only retired when she reached the age of sixty in 1993.

As Andy has said, Religion was very important to Mum

Andy and Mum Helen, Christmas 2007

and she told us when she was young, that she wanted to become a Nun and join a Convent. If she had, we would not be here today, which, Peter says; "I reflect on this at times and as my children have grown, I have told them the decisions they make now would 'map the path for the rest of their lives'."

Peter continues; "Mum enjoyed evening art classes at the primary school we attended and, although she didn't particularly like sport, she fully and happily accepted it as part of her life, washing football kits, making teas, cakes and sandwiches for the cricket team and staying at home as Andy, Dad and I went to away matches."

"Mum was also a keen gardener and enjoyed maintaining our improvised cricket and football pitch! It amazes me, and I know that Andy feels the same, that how adaptable Mum was, at being able to join in our games and play in the garden, often bowling under-arm with a tennis ball. She also had an uncanny ability to catch the ball returned at speed to her in a 'snapping fashion'." Peter continues;

Hackney Marshes football pitches

"I suppose years of practice with two boys to occupy her had something to do with that!"

Andy and Peter both reminisce about their father, with Peter saying; "Dad was sport-driven; he was heavily involved in the cricket club, which was just a short walk away from the houses in Bury and Felixstowe. I recall him having frantic telephone calls on a Friday night, trying to get a team together for the weekend fixtures." Andy continues; "Dad was never short of a game and often played midweek if he could get the time off. Winter season was football and then later on indoor cricket."

John played football on Sunday mornings when Peter and Andy were both young and then on Sunday afternoons for a Customs and Excise team. Peter recalls John telling him and Andy that when he was in London, he played four times at the weekend. Saturday morning, then once more in the afternoon and the same again on Sunday, on Hackney Marshes, which is internationally known as the spiritual home of Sunday league football, with 82 football, rugby and cricket pitches on North and South Marsh and Mabley Green.[7]

Peter recalls; "Later on, we all played football together for Felixstowe Juniors. Andy was twenty and working, I was sixteen and Dad was in is fifties! While we were at Primary School Dad helped to start up a football team at the school."

Andy's father John, in his cricket whites

1 St. Albans Football Team 1976/77
Back Row: Mark Scott P.E, Michael Baroni, Simon Sidani, Paul Johnson, Michael McAteer, Patrick Scanlon, Unknown
Front Row: Rob Simpson, Kenny Lawler, Andrew Kelway, Andy (Captain), Mark Ward, Pat Aldridge, Pat Shearing

1977/78 St. Albans School Cricket Team. Andy (Captain) 2nd from the right, front row

As has been discussed earlier, Helen's Catholicism was extremely important to her, so much, so that John converted to Catholicism in order to marry her in 1958. She encouraged the boys to attend church regularly in the hope that their interest in the church would blossom. To her delight, they became altar boys and joined the Catholic youth club connected with their local church.

Up to the time that the family moved from Bury St Edmunds, Andy was a pupil at St. Edmunds Roman Catholic Primary School in Westgate Street. Helen and John were very particular about where the boys went to school and they agreed that a Roman Catholic school was essential in order to ensure that the boys maintained their religious education.

St Edmunds R.C Primary School, in Bury St Edmunds.

When the family moved to Felixstowe, both boys attended the Convent of Jesus & Mary, on Orwell Rd, Felixstowe. At the age of sixteen, nearing seventeen, Andy left home and, although he had been a regular churchgoer with his Mother, he made the decision that he didn't want to attend church any longer. He, in his own words, rebelled. He wanted to express himself fully, he wanted to explore and not just the world.... he needed to discover something. Who was he?

He knew that he wanted his own money, he had been very fortunate to have had a stable, loving and comfortable childhood into his teens. Like the majority of adolescent teenagers, he wanted a car and money so that he could afford to go out at the weekends with friends. "Mum and I had very similar personalities" Andy recalls; "which meant that on the odd occasion we'd disagree about something and as a young adolescent man growing up, I wanted independence. I wanted a driving licence; you know girlfriends and things like that. I just wanted to take control of my life".

"Dad would give me lessons and I became quite adept at driving at quite a young age, so much so, that I would drive Peter on his paper round in Dad's Mazda 626". Andy continued; "I had driving lessons booked with a driving school for the week following my seventeenth birthday and I took my test in Ipswich four months later. One thing I remember about the test, being in second gear on the hill start and hoping that the examiner hadn't noticed. I continued as if nothing had happened and passed the first time. That episode taught me so much about not getting flustered and thinking on my feet."

Andy's first introduction to the world of work was a period of work experience in an office on Felixstowe Docks. Helen arranged this after one of her neighbours told her about the position. The job involved Andy carrying out very basic duties, which included filing, making coffee and other very modest office duties. "It was a really good starter role for me"; Andy says; "and it gave me the opportunity to learn about office administration, which was really useful when I applied for my first real job, which was at HRG Group (HRG), the Government freight agents in Felixstowe.

Brothers-in-law Francis Hogg, a young wine merchant and Augustus Robinson, an insurance broker founded the

Group in 1845. Their web page describes HRG thus. 'From our origins as a City of London insurance firm to the global business we are today, our company has adapted successfully to the ever-changing needs of corporate customers for more than 170 years.'

On Stonegrove Road in Felixstowe and just a stone's throw from the docks stands two large grey and white six-storey office blocks. Housed within these buildings, Trelawney House, were the offices of HRG, the Government Freight Agents. Andy explains that any Government Freight that entered or left the country had to go through an HRG Freight Agency.

Because Andy had a driving license, HRG employed him as a Dock Runner. He would take the documents from the office to the Customs House or from the Customs House down to the dock face and deliver paperwork variously around the dock. Andy was seventeen when he started and he grew to;

"...absolutely love the job". Working within a small team of six people with, as Andy recalls;" ...a great boss called Bill Wilkes. He took me under his wing and he was a terrific teacher and mentor."

Andy continues; "There was a kind of dock runner's gang, if you like, a small community of runners, all with cars and there was a certain amount of 'car envy' between us. We were a tight-knit group and we would race around the docks trying to deliver the paperwork and documents in the fastest possible time. We would all look out for each other and if one of us was in trouble, or needed help, we'd be there.

Andy continued to do the dock runner's job for about two years, whilst simultaneously learning about all of the other rôles within the office. Eventually, the company employed someone to replace him as dock runner, promoted him to office clerk, and then after four or five years, promoted him to office supervisor and in charge of the team.

Andy continues; "When Bill, the office Manager Bill was away, I started to take on more responsibility and as it was a national company I was required to travel regularly to

London. This travel and the contacts, which I made, exposed me to some excellent opportunities in London as well; it was a brilliant stepping stone for me personally."

Andy remembers the introduction of computers and this started to cancel out the need to hand write all of the customers' documentation. Because of this, his typing became quite fast, accurate, and later, nearer to the time when he ended his career with HRG the company began to network the computer system and link directly through the embryonic internet to customers. It was still all new and represented another steep learning curve for Andy and one, which true to his nature he faced head-on and seized with both hands. He was now starting to earn good money and spending it as quickly as he made it. "I liked clothes and having the latest things and I wanted a car so that my best friend Chris and I could get out and about more. I also wanted the car to reflect my personality so I bought a blue Mark1 1.6 Capri K-registration, which cost me, I think, about two hundred pounds. It probably was worth about £100 if you were to value it against how safe it was. I recall once whilst travelling down the A12 after a night out at the Tartan House nightclub in Frating all the lights went out whilst travelling at 70mph!

Chris and I went out often, up to London and the nightclubs and out as far as Essex. Pretty soon, though, I sold that car to a mate and bought another Capri Mark 2." Peter remembers that it was; *".... a bright blue M-registration with black louvre rear window, front spoiler, alloy wheels and twin square headlights. It also had a Clarion stereo and speakers."* Andy recalls that one night, driving out up to the West End, the lights on the car cut out. That was his and Chris' night spoilt as Andy had to turn around and go back home again.

Andy sold the Capri on for a profit and bought a Triumph TR7 R-registration in red with a yellow and black stripe down the side of the body. Peter remembers it was a nice car.

Tartan house Nightclub in Frating, Colchester

Andy felt that he had "made it" when he bought the Triumph. He has always preferred the sportier, faster cars and two other cars he bought reflected this, a G-registration Golf GTI and an M-registration Fiesta XR2. Both brothers liked their cars, as Peter also had a green MG Metro and a red Ford Escort.

Andy's first 'Sports' car

Andy now drives an impressive black VW Golf TDI. His dream car though, is a Graphite grey Range Rover Sport.

He was quite spendthrift during the time he worked at HRG but he certainly enjoyed his life. He soon

A fine example of a Graphite Grey Range Rover Sport, reproduced courtesy © Overfinch

began spending more than he was earning but one day, he doesn't remember when he had a 'Road to Damascus' moment and he made a conscious decision; "…to make sure that I managed my money appropriately…" That decision changed his life and he has been very careful with his money to the point of being, as he would say, frugal.

Andy had left home by the time he started working at HRG, albeit only a couple of hundred yards from his Mother and although by then he had stopped attending church regularly, he knew that religion was always going to be there for him. He is quite resolute in his faith, saying; "…. whether it's right or wrong. Whenever I've needed religion I know it's there for me; I mean times where - you know I sat down and prayed; there have been times through adversity where I need that support and it has been a good crutch for me to lean on, it's helped me through the death of my parents, there's no doubt about that." When discussing the delicate matter of his parents' death and in response to me asking if he ever questioned the validity of a God or reincarnation after death; "No, it's the opposite, it gives me comfort knowing I will see them again in heaven." So how does he reconcile his faith with his desire to become a Royal Marine? "So, for me - it was a difficult thing for me to join the Marines and know that someday I might kill someone. One thing I gravitated towards was, is that there is good in life and there's bad in life and as long as you're ensuring that good can succeed over evil then that's OK; besides I couldn't kill anybody in cold blood." When he was asked, "But what if somebody were pointing a rifle at you then? Andy continued; "Well yeah, I would be in that situation, having to return fire on them. I think we're quite good in this country ensuring that we're not doing things for the sake of doing it, but there's been some good rationale behind justifying action against people."

Andy had considered joining the Marines at 16 or 17 years of age but he says - and is quite adamant - that he did not think he had the stamina or strength at that young age. Peter disagrees with his brother, saying that he thinks he did not join because he had such a good job and was enjoying his life too much.

Both brothers had been members of church youth clubs as youngsters as well as the Cubs and Scout troops. Andy later joined the Air Cadets and Peter became a Sea Cadet. Peter recalls Andy discussing the Royal Marines with him in 1979 when Andy was about 15; this would probably have been around the time when Andy was in the Air Cadets. Peter, being just 11 at the time probably would not have been able to envisage life in the Marines but he remembers it left an impression on him. Both boys would have been exposed to a quasi-regimental structure while in their respective Cadet Troops so to want to continue that into adult life would be, I suppose, a natural progression. However, Andy decided for whatever reason to postpone his entry into the Royal Marines.

Some of Andy's sporting badges

--o0o---

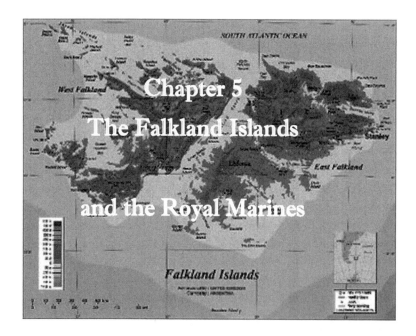

Chapter 5

The Falkland Islands and the Royal Marines

Whatever one's views of the politics of the conflict, there is not a scintilla of doubt that the brave and courageous Royal Marines achieved something truly breath-taking by defeating the Argentine forces in just ten weeks. It certainly does take a special person to want to become - and then succeed as a Royal Marine.

The Forces Network wrote an article asking; "Who are the Royal Marines?"

The Royal Marines describe themselves as 'The world's most elite amphibious fighting force'[1]. Technically, they are part of the Royal Navy, although they see themselves as completely separate. They are trained to respond rapidly to international crises. They are also trained to be deadly. What sort of person actually has what it takes to become one of these super-soldiers?

To start with, every individual hoping to become a Royal Marine Commando must undertake a gruelling 32-weeks 'basic training' course. With it being the longest infantry training in NATO, it is fair to say that the Commando course is anything but basic. The course ends with the infamous 30-mile 'yomp' across Dartmoor, carrying full battle kit weighing 32lbs. The yomp is probably one of the most physically challenging tests to exist in any military. Sadly, the physical demands of the exercise caused the death of one young recruit back in 2015, which led to calls for relaxing the training but the force maintained that this was what was required to turn a civilian into a Royal Marines Commando.

Before they reach that point, they have to learn to live, breathe, eat and clean like a Royal Marine, in effect, husbandry. The philosophy of 'husbandry' is that if you can't make your bed or polish your boots properly, then how can the other Commandos in combat rely upon you? During training, the unit drills the Commando values of excellence, integrity, self-discipline and humility into recruits.

Along with this, the Royal Marines teach trainees to embody the Commando qualities of determination, courage, unselfishness and cheerfulness in the face of adversity, and the all-important 'commando mind-set': 'be the first to understand; the first to adapt and respond, and the first to overcome'.

The average Royal Marine recruit can expect to receive around 4-6 hours of sleep per night; there's a reason that they're known as 'nods'. Owing to a combination of huge physical exertion and sleep deprivation, recruits will frequently 'nod off'. It's no wonder that 40% of Royal Marine recruits drop out before the end of the 32-week training from homesickness or other "professional issues". Many also suffer serious injuries that prevent them from finishing the course.

So why does anyone want to apply? Forces Network's Cassidy Little[2] decided to join the Royal Marines after being told by a friend; "Everybody respects a failure; nobody respects a quitter. At least as a failure, you gave it your best." He said: "It's the longest and hardest basic training in the world…their current slogan was 99.9% need not apply. "Everybody including myself had no expectation of me succeeding.

"They literally teach you from the very basics - how to iron something, how to wash, how to make your bed, how to use a knife and fork, how to brush your teeth. If you can't be trusted to maintain your own teeth, how can you be trusted to manage a weapons system?"

"For the first four weeks, you're not allowed to quit. They've spent so much money getting you to that point; they want you to have a good go at it before they send you home.

"Our final graduation group had 13 of the original 54 guys. "It was tough, but it should be tough." There is no doubt that it takes a special sort of person to become a Royal Marines Commando; as the force tells potential recruits on its website: "There's one thing that all our people share. That special state of mind. It is the foundation of life in the Royal Marines. To prove you have it you'll need to demonstrate certain qualities, every day."[9]

Peter and Andy surely are both very special people. Peter joined the Marines as a junior in 1984 and he recalls; "When I joined it was only a couple of years after the Falklands War. This is the first Conflict where as a youngster it had left an impression on me with the artists' drawings from the war and the grainy news footage. And the iconic photos of 45 Commando yomping across the Falklands and the Marines raising the Union

Jack at Port Stanley following the surrender of the Argentine Forces." These images were so powerful. Would Peter have joined had not he and his brother discussed the Marines when he was just 11 or 12? I'll leave that one hanging there…

Peter left the Marines in January 1995 having served just over ten years. In August 1992, he married his wife Joanne. They have two children, Christian and Bethany.

Andy and Peter's father John, passed away on the 1st May 2008 of a Cerebrovascular Accident or Stroke and Peter offered the following as a tribute to his father.

"Cricket was his love and when Andy and Dad played first-team cricket I often had to make up the numbers when they were short and became quite good at fielding but it was good to play in the same team together. Dad was brought up in St John's Wood and he always talked about Lord's and how he spent all his days there playing on the nursery ground. I paid lip service to this knowing now what it is like to get into any sports ground let alone Lord's. However, I went with Dad to watch Andy play for the Combined Services against Young England at Lord's. This was my first visit to Lord's and I was watching my brother play there. The ground was empty, which meant we could move around the different stands as the game progressed. We went into the seating adjacent to the pavilion, which was the members' stand. A steward was stood at the front we sat down on some chairs. I was astonished; we had been there a couple of minutes when the elderly steward came across and said that he remembered Dad from when he was a young lad. I thought to myself that all those stories about Lord's were true after all!

Dad was a generous person. He always gave us encouragement and pushed us to excel in everything we did. He loved his sport; he loved Arsenal football club, Middlesex and the Australian test team. Although Dad was quite ill when Andy was first involved in Somerset Cricket, he was so proud of him and we were able to watch the One-Day cup final against Yorkshire in 2002 at Lord's."

Peter and Andy had, in their opinion, the very best role models anybody could want. Characteristics, which John and Helen passed on to their two boys, including determination, the strength of character, fairness, honesty and integrity have made Peter and Andy the men they are now. Jacob is already showing some of these characteristics and with his father as his mentor, his future is promising.

It is perhaps, self-evident that Peter (and his wife) have passed on some of that grit to Christian and Bethany and they both have glittering and successful career paths ahead.

---o0o---

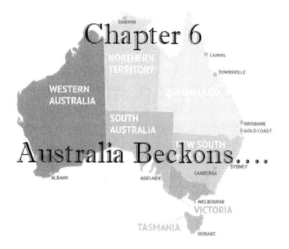

Chapter 6

Australia Beckons....

Chapter 6

Australia Beckons...

It was 1986. Andy was 22 and holding down a successful

position at HRG, where he had been employed for about five years. He had advanced through the various roles within the company to where he

Andy's first house in Trimley-St-Mary

now occupied the position of office supervisor and was assuming the office manager's position in his absence. In time, HRG employed more members of staff and they invited Andy to set up and manage an office off-site. Fairly soon Andy was running a satellite office at RAF Brize Norton.

Andy bought a two bedroomed terrace house and it seemed that his life was mapped out for him. He was young; he had a nice car, good friends. He was careful with money.... had he reached 'Nirvana'?

Being an office manager suited his personality. He was sober, reliable and trustworthy…. but he was a young man.

He asked himself the perennial question, which everybody asks at least once in his or her life; "Who am I"?

Interestingly, Psychology Today© answers the question in this way; "The emphasis shouldn't be on discovering who you are (what is buried beneath) but on facilitating the emergence of what you'd like to experience."[1]

It is a truism that we all live 'sedimentary' lives and each experience layers and enhances our perception and understanding of self and makes for a more rounded person….in the majority of cases, it has to be said.

Nevertheless, eighteen months after buying his house in Trimley St. Mary, on the outskirts of Felixstowe it had appreciated significantly enough for him to consider selling for a tidy profit and fulfil a dream, which had been bubbling under for some months… to set off to explore Australia.

Andy tells me; "A very good friend of mine, Chris Wolkenstein, with whom I've been friends from the age of eleven, also worked in the shipping business while I was at HRG. He now runs his own business in New

Jersey. He decided that he wanted to go to Australia as well, so we set a date and agreed that we would make firm plans when we arrived in Oz. We had shared a flat together at one time but now had our own houses."

It took Chris a bit longer to sell his house but as Andy had already bought his ticket, he made the decision to travel on his own and Chris said that he would follow.

He flew with Cathay Pacific to Melbourne, via Hong Kong, and his Auntie and cousin met him at the airport. They drove the 29 miles back to their house on Whitehaven Street, Wyndham Vale, Werribee, in-between Geelong and Melbourne. The quiet street where they lived comprised tidy, well-maintained one-storey properties, all with neat, manicured lawns abutting onto the road.

Andy's Auntie Josephine was a telephonist and Uncle Ray had been an Officer in the Royal Australian Air Force. His cousin Christopher Rae Bassett was a youth worker. He stayed with them for a few weeks, while he waited for his friend Chris to arrive, acclimatising himself, all the while deciding what he wanted to do when he and Chris would meet up again.

Eventually, Chris sold his house and flew out to Sydney to stay with his cousin's family and the story now gets interesting so I'm going to let Andy 'tell' it; "…. You know, I think it was an adventure and I was excited but at the same time a bit apprehensive. I didn't really know what was going to happen. However, you know I wasn't going out there completely blind, I had arranged to meet up with my Auntie Josephine and her husband Ray and I stayed with them for the first few weeks, maybe a month, while I looked to make a bit of a plan to go and look round Australia.

One of my cousins, Chris Rae Bassett, is quite a lot older

A typical example of the houses on Whitehaven Street

than me. He was married and had a house around the corner [in Burgundy Drive] and my Aunt and family were going to go away on holiday to Bali.

My cousin Chris said I could stay in his house and look after it, while they were away and I said that would be great. So, I rang my mate Chris and told him to fly down to Melbourne. Chris had lent me his car so I arranged to pick him up. I was very lucky, as I was able to stay in Chris Rae's house.

Chris arrived, I picked him up and he stayed with me in my cousin's house. We travelled around in my cousin's car, doing bits and pieces around Geelong and then we saw an advert for Falls Creek, a ski resort on the border of New South Wales and Victoria.

We thought right, we're going for the weekend so we decided we were going to drive, so we took my cousin's car up to the mountains.

We had to purchase some snow chains and we stayed there for the weekend.... we absolutely loved it, absolutely loved it. It was quite an adventure driving up there because I'd never driven in snow before and actually, it was quite risky.

While we were up at Falls Creek, we'd made a couple of contacts and coming back we thought; you know what, we're going to try and get some jobs. We got hold of them and said; "are there any opportunities for employment" and they said, "yeah, come on up!"

My cousin and aunt were still away on holiday while this was all going on so I came back, packed up everything we wanted, left the car and left the house.

I let my Aunt know that we were going off to go and work in Falls Creek ski resort. Chris and I caught the train up to the mountains and we started work up there......BUT I MADE A BIG MISTAKE. In retrospect, a BIG mistake!

I left the house in a terrible order, I left food in the fridge, left the beds unmade and I hadn't swept anywhere. All the food had gone off and my cousin has come home, you know he's very disappointed in me and there's a horrendous smell in the fridge. I had never really looked after myself up to that point and you know I hadn't cleaned the toilets and left it how I found it and he was unhappy with me understandably and so was my Aunt at the time; she wrote me a letter saying how disappointed she was in me. One of the most disappointing things is that you know I didn't ask permission to take their car to Falls Creek in the snow. Looking back, it was poor judgement from me; I had abused their hospitality, the whole thing was a massive learning experience for me. However, I was young and you learn from it and I definitely have done - thinking back on it retrospectively. We had been selfish; I was young and I was quite naive in thinking I could drive a car up to the mountains in snow. I'd put their car at risk and us at risk also. It was all about us and we didn't consider anybody else. We got to Falls Creek and we worked up there for a number of months. I worked as a waiter in the restaurant at the top of the mountain and Chris was working as a barman living on-site in the staff accommodation - and the reason we were doing this was that we could get free skiing and I learned how to ski, only basic stuff. It was a great time - unbelievable and there are so many workers; diverse groups, it was cosmopolitan, from all around the world. Once we finished work in the day and skied back down the mountain, we'd get all our food provided for and then we just party all night and wake up with a stinking headache and a hangover the next day. It was phenomenal, absolutely phenomenal and we had built some really good relationships with people out there who were travelling as well. Then while we're out there, we met a guy who was from New Zealand; he was ex-New Zealand army and he was going to go and do some work in another resort up at the Great Barrier Reef called Great Keppel Island.

It was like an 18-30 resort on the Barrier Reef and he said; "you know you guys should consider coming and working there" and that's how that network of travellers works.

You make contacts, you just move around and use those contacts to get other employment opportunities, and so we decided that's what we're going to do next. So, we left Falls Creek; we had this money from selling our houses, so we got on a Greyhound Bus and we made our way up to Brisbane and then on to the Gold Coast.

Great Keppel Island is a half-hour ferry ride from Yeppoon, approximately halfway up the Queensland coast and 20 miles northeast of Rockhampton. Rockhampton (sometimes shortened to Rocky), which straddles the Tropic of Capricorn is a major transport hub, with plane and bus connections to Brisbane and other cities. Lonely Planet[1] describes it thus: 'Rocky can be aptly scorching. It's 40 km inland and lacks coastal sea breezes and summers are often unbearably humid. The town has a smattering of attractions but is best seen as a gateway to the coastal gems of Yeppoon and Great Keppel Island, and the Byfield National Park to the north.'

We joined up on the ferry across the Great Barrier Reef, booked ourselves a hotel room....and we were only planning to be there for a long weekend with a view to finding jobs later but found employment straight away. We didn't go back, you know; we moved into the staff

Andy's Falls Creek Pass

accommodation and then we started working there and I worked as a waiter and it was phenomenal, brilliant and it's amazing what happens when you're away and you're travelling, you know. It was brilliant for me to get to know another group of people. But if you can just visualise an idyllic island and the Great Barrier Reef.

I'm getting up, I'm serving breakfast and lunch or lunch and dinner because you do two shifts out of three, then the rest of the time you're free to go sunbathing or enjoy the water sports on the unbelievably crystal-clear waters on the Barrier Reef.

So, I worked as a waiter for a while and then the resort D.J. left. There as a nightclub on the island and he used to play there. They couldn't get anybody to replace him so

A typical Great Keppel Ferry   *A Greyhound bus of the period*

they said to me; you're from England, I mean you got some good tunes; could you DJ temporarily"? I agreed to stand in.

And so, I left being a waiter thinking that I always knew I could go back to it and there I was doing the D.J. job, starting at ten o'clock at night and finishing at three o'clock in the morning and the rest of the time I had off. It was the best job in the world, I mean *really* the best job in the world and it was my job to play tunes. Then there'd be a break where a live band would come on and then I'd play some more and another break for the live band and then

I'd finished the evening off and it was just brilliant being at the centre of this hub of activity of people on holiday…..party central.

I used to lie on the beach, snorkel, sail or exercise in the gym. I was living the dream, but like anything, it became a bit Groundhog Day and became a bit repetitive and after six weeks, I actually got bored with it. I was thinking about doing something else and I decided then that I have got to move on, so I handed in my notice, said my goodbyes, jumped on the ferry and the Greyhound bus again and made my way down to Sydney.

Eventually I met up with Chris and we decided to travel again. We went back up to the Gold Coast with a view to travel up to the Northern Territories. We were sat on the beach one day there on the Gold Coast and this guy approached us and said; "I'm looking for a couple of guys to work on my yacht and I'm looking to sail it from here up to Darwin. Are you interested"? Without hesitation, Chris and I both said yes, together!

We worked on this guy's sixty-five-foot Ketch for a number of weeks, sailing up and down the Barrier Reef. It was unbelievable, just him and his wife; he was the captain and we were just doing general duties. He was charging other people to ferry them from A to B anywhere up the coast; although we didn't get a wage they looked after us and we were ultimately going to get free passage to Darwin at the end of it. We got to a point where he was training us up to be able to work the sails; training us up to be able to sail at night using the charts with the compass, to the point where he and his wife could get their heads down and Chris and I could share the navigating through the night. It was brilliant, really good. We did that for a number of weeks"; he grins; "not sure if I could do

Andy at the helm of the Ketch

it now.

There was a lot of technology on the boat, which allowed us to make sure we kept on course and in waters, deep enough, where there's no threat from running it aground.

I had wanted to go up to the Northern Territories because it's completely different up there.

If you want to experience all of Australia, you've got to try to get around as much as you possibly can and so we ended up getting off the Ketch at Darwin, after sailing across to the Cape of Capricorn Coast it was a phenomenal experience for us.

We landed in Darwin and compared to the land we had left down in Queensland, compared to the land that we'd been used to up to then it was like chalk and cheese, just phenomenal. It was so dry and it's…just orange; the whole place is just orange and the people there have a completely different mind-set". [Author's note] *Some Aussies view the Top End as 'The Wild West', as it is known colloquially. It's a tropical region, which lies less than a thousand miles from the equator.*

Mickie Southam an indigenous Aussie summed Darwin up like so; "Darwin for me was bloody horrible but I am not a hot weather person. It has two seasons, the wet and the dry. The weather is tolerable, barely, between seasons, but during the wet, everything that can grow mould will. Even things you thought could not possibly get mouldy do. Then in the dry, the mould all disappears and everything that was covered in the mould is coated in a thick layer of dust instead. The smallest scratch or bite can turn into a tropical ulcer, which is really nasty".

Andy and Chris in the Australian Bush

But another native 'top-end' Aussie, Shereem writes; "The things we love most about living in the Top End include: The endless summer; the relaxed atmosphere; It's quite family friendly; the small-town feel; the amazing natural environment - including the contrasting "seasons" i.e. the wet and dry, and the incredible lightning displays.) Andy continues; "I'm glad I experienced the Top End. Anyhow, Chris decided that he was going to catch the Greyhound bus back down to Sydney but I'd decided that I would hitchhike back through the middle. I hitched a ride on a road train, which is basically an articulated lorry with three, four or five twenty-foot trailers on the back of it and this bloke gave me a lift all the way back down. That was another phenomenal experience; all the way down, about two thousand seven hundred miles, seeing the real Australia. We went through Burrundie, Pine Creek, brushing past Nitmiluk National Park, St Katherine's Gorge, where there are 'salties' (saltwater crocodiles), ospreys and cockatoos. Past Elsey National Park with its thermal pools and dingoes. At Warumungu we travelled east out of the Northern Territory into Queensland, down into New South Wales and the Blue Mountains and finally into Sydney.

It took maybe ten or eleven days, which I suppose is quite a long time. I fell out a number of times with the driver on that trip but again it was another great experience and I had to learn to get on with this true-blue Aussie; he was a proper roughneck but it was a great time to be alive, it was phenomenal. I had to learn to live in a confined space; basically, in someone's shoes and we were living, eating and sleeping in the back of the cab. Back in Sydney, I met up with my best friend Chris and stayed with him for a

An Australian 'road-train'

week or so and we socialised with friends we had met in Great Keppel Island.

We decided to stay in Sydney and rent a flat in Glebe, a suburb of Sydney and about 3 miles west of the Sydney Harbour Bridge and the iconic Opera House.

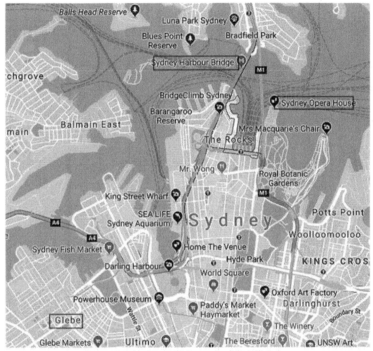

Glebe, where Andy and Chris stayed, while in Sydney

We rented some furniture and enjoyed what Sydney had to offer a couple of young blokes. However, it wasn't long before we were struggling financially, so we had to find ways to raise money and pay the rent.

As hard as we tried, we could not find any regular jobs and in desperation, we bought two buckets, sponges and some washing up liquid. We made our way down to a major intersection in the city and every time the lights turned red, we burst out onto the road and washed windscreens, then begged for a dollar.

We gave a few free washes when we were told in no uncertain terms to '…go away'. Even though the days were very long, we made good money and it kept a roof over our head, food on the table and importantly enough, spare cash to ensure we maintained our social activities. Having said that, we did become very effective at not spending money and 'experts' at 'mine-sweeping' drinks….

From Darwin, if Andy had wanted to travel south to Adelaide instead of Sydney, he could have travelled on the 26 carriage 'Ghan'.

The train journey that scythes the country in half for over eighteen hundred and fifty miles and, which is purportedly named after the Afghan camel drivers who arrived in Australia in the late 19th century, to help the British colonisers find a way to reach the country's interior.[2]

There are, however, conflicting opinions of this, inasmuch that some historians claim that the name was an oblique insult. Legend has it that, when in 1891, the steam-driven locomotive travelled from Quorn and reached remote

Oodnadatta, there lived an itinerant population of around 150 cameleers, who were called colloquially "Afghans".

It is claimed that "The Ghan Express" name originated as early as 1924; owing to the notorious unreliability of the fortnightly steam train, European sheep and cattle farmers commonly called it *"...in ribald fashion, The Afghan Express"*.[3]

By 1951, when diesel-electric locomotives replaced steam engines, the journey was more reliable and indeed the Great Southern Railway now prides itself on the excellent standard of the service offered to its passengers.

The train can travel for two days without seeing another living person but, if the train breaks down, the company has to carry out a repair 'en route'....and as most of the journey is single track; a replacement locomotive is not always an option.

It takes 54 hours to travel the 1,851 miles with a four-hour stopover in Alice Springs.[4] and it has to be one of the world's most picturesque journeys, which takes in some of the most beautiful but also some of the most remote places on earth.

If you want to travel on The Ghan, expect to pay upwards of A$1500 for the journey from Adelaide to Darwin depending on the standard of travel. Great Southern Railway also runs the Indian Pacific train twice each week from Perth to Sydney via Kalgoorlie and Adelaide.

The Original Ghan Express 1924

A Diesel locomotive of the period

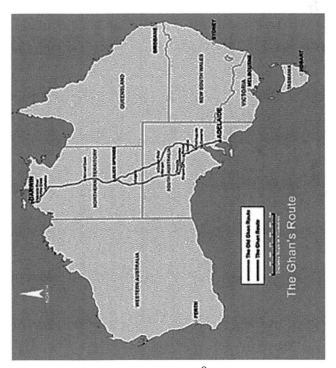

Darwin
Katherine
Tennant Creek
Alice Springs
Kulgera
Northern Territory border
South Australia
Chandler
Marla
Coober Pedy (Manguri)
Indian Pacific from Perth
Indian Pacific to Perth
Tarcoola
Kingoonya
Pimba
Port Augusta
Indian Pacific to Sydney
Coonamia near Port Pirie
Adelaide

The Ghan's Route

---oOo---

Andy and Royal Marines colleagues in Norway extreme cold weather training

Andy and Royal marines Colleagues in Iraq 1991

Andy in Iraq 1991, showing his friendly face for the local children

A proud Andy receiving his Royal Marines cap and badge

Andy in full kit and camouflage face paint

A proud man at the pinnacle as a Royal Marine

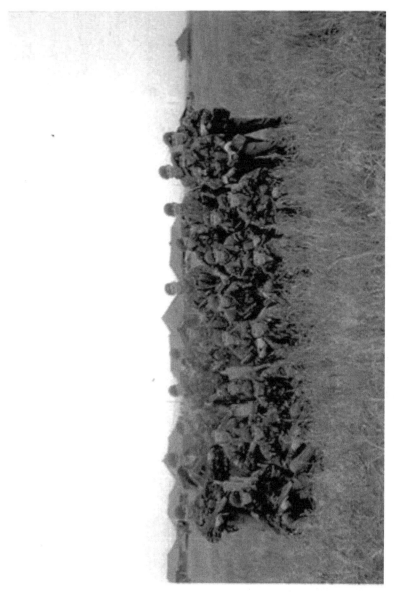

Charlie Company in Southern Turkey, before being air-lifted by helicopter into Northern Iraq in 1991. Andy is in the middle row, kneeling 3rd from the right

Chapter 7

By Land, By Sea Royal Marines

During the time that Andy and Chris were navigating their separate ways around Australia, Peter was in Belize with the Marines. George Allison writes[1] in the UK Defence Journal that; "Howler monkeys, tarantulas, black widow spiders and snakes; …just some of the residents who have 'welcomed' Royal Marines to the jungle of Belize this week. The Royal Marine Commandos are putting all their basic soldiering skills to the test as they learn to fight and survive in one of the world's most hostile environments".

"Commandos in Belize conduct vital training under the watchful eye of the British Army Training Support Unit Belize (BATSUB)[2] and The Royal Marines directing staff"

The first phase of training involves the Royal Marines conducting break contact drills (the platoon or squad must continue to suppress the enemy as it breaks contact), close target reconnaissance, survival, patrol and navigation training in the depths of Sibun Gorge.

Meanwhile, the BATSUB staff, called trackers, teach the elite Commandos all about operating in the jungle; providing instruction on survival, building shelters and animal traps, creating fire, and understanding what plants are edible, inedible and which are medicinal, as well as what insects and wildlife to avoid in this environment.

The website, www.guidetobelize.info has some smart advice; "Keeping a level head and an awareness of your surroundings will keep you alive if you

use a few simple safety procedures. Do not let curiosity and carelessness kill or injure you".

There are a plethora of snakes, arachnids, insects and other larger animal species, some of which may not be immediately visible but, which can inflict a nasty bite. These include, on land –

Black Widow Spider; its venom is 15 times as poisonous as the venom of the rattlesnake.

Bullet Ant; its powerful and potent venom is said to be as painful as being shot with a bullet. It is called by the locals "Hormiga Veinticuatro" or "24-hour ant", from the 24 hours of pain that follow a stinging.

Brown Recluse Spider; you may not realise that you have been stung but a redness and itchiness is followed by necrotising of the skin and gangrene.

The Coral Snake, the **Dart Frog** and several other species of snake and reptile inhabit the rainforest.

The Keel Billed Toucan, a large brightly coloured parrot is the national bird of Belize and there are several other

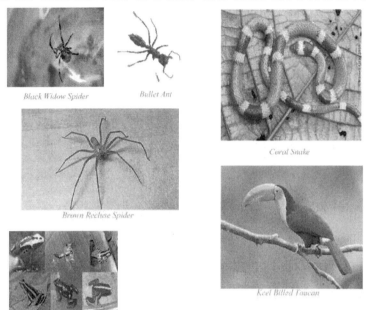

Black Widow Spider   Bullet Ant

Coral Snake

Brown Recluse Spider

Keel Billed Toucan

Dart Frogs

species of totally harmless and stunning bird and wildlife species including colourful butterflies and hummingbirds, as can be seen at the Green Hills Butterfly Ranch, Mile 8 Pine Ridge Road, Belize.

The ranch has hummingbird feeders, which as several people have commented on, attract '…. all kinds of colourful hummingbirds.

Of course, Andy himself would be going out to jungle training in Guyana and the West Indies with the Royal

Marines in due course, as he too would progress through the additional arduous training regime to become a full-fledged jungle and arctic warfare trained elite Royal Marine. Both Andy and Peter would end their careers as 'elite' Physical Training Instructors (PTI).

The Royal Marines initially drafted Andy to 40 Commando Logistics Regiment, CTCRM Lympstone and then ended his career at Norton Manor Camp.

Elite is a clichéd word and we use it too freely to describe the dull, ordinary and mundane in our 'celebrity' world. Indeed, Jacques Peretti, an award-winning BBC investigative reporter and Guardian journalist, sums this up quite nicely. 'Once upon a time, elites were revered to the same degree they are distrusted today. They also had another name: experts…But now the word "expert" has become the derogatory "elite."' Consequently, it has in popular culture, lost its true meaning. It is a fact, also, that the English language evolves and words, which a generation ago conveyed some gravitas, are now used colloquially and as such are 'dumbed down'.

To become a true 'elite', the Royal Navy requires that candidates hold the rank of Corporal, even before consideration for enrolment into the Royal Marines Physical Training Branch. The Army is different inasmuch that a candidate can be a rank below, a Lance Corporal.

PTIs are primarily responsible for making sure would-be Marines meet the physical requirements of the Corps; identifying their strengths and weaknesses throughout the 32-week training course at the Commando Training Centre Royal Marines (CTCRM).

Course Instructor Sergeant Mo Morris writes in 2014; "After 17 weeks of intensive training, during which they received instruction in combat conditioning, anatomy, physiology and nutrition, gained qualifications including swimming pool life guard, boxing, cricket, basketball, volleyball and rugby league coaching, four green berets became physical training instructors (PTI).

So, Andy qualified as a PTI, where the grades are Fail, Pass and Superior and he qualified with a Superior Pass. Andy's Chief of Staff at CTCRM, Mike Hill, wrote glowingly of Andy; "Whilst serving as Chief of Staff at the CTCRM I did have the good fortune to have Andy on the staff as one of some thirty or so instructors who were involved with the day-to-day training and development of potential Royal Marines.

This was a difficult job for me as there was a culture in place where no quarter is given for error, sloppiness or anything that came close to less than excellent standards of instruction and performance, from anyone. I can honestly say that Andy was one of a small band of instructors who could always be thoroughly relied upon to complete any given task and was all the more impressive as he managed to combine all the physical attributes required, with a positive mental attitude, which made him stand out that little bit more.

Mike recalls sending for him one day to explain that the local University at Exeter had an art department and were willing to pay for the services of a well-defined male model to pose for one of their regular classes and that some level of nudity may be involved. He said that Andy's eyes lit up at this and whilst Mike wasn't too sure what his reaction would be at the time, Andy was "off like a rat up a trouser leg"!

Mike has said that he is not surprised that Andy's career has had such a level of success and he suggests that there may something in the 'family genes' as his brother Peter was also a PT Instructor and was also a very high calibre individual and it is self-evident that Andy leaves an indelible mark on everyone he meets.

Andy enjoyed many tours with the Marines and relished the opportunity to travel all round the world with the Corps.

After serving three winters in Norway, he earned the right to call himself a Military Ski Instructor and pass on the special skills in order to survive and fight in the harshest arctic conditions.

As has been mentioned previously, he trained to fight in the jungle, an experience that is lowest on his list of pleasures and Andy stresses that the ability to keep himself clean was a stretch at best as the jungle was a 'honking' environment. The desert was also challenging as water was at such a premium and the sand used to play havoc with the operational use of his weapon.

Even though Andy had reached the rank of Corporal and PTI Superior, at heart he was a Royal Marine Combat Soldier. He wanted to finish his career as he had started it, as a combat soldier. He tendered his eighteen months' notice and requested to be stationed back to 40 Commando at Taunton Manor Camp and eventually returned to Charlie Company as a Section Corporal, with the responsibility as a qualified PTI, to manage his Company's fitness, which, as Andy recounts; "I relished, managing sixty to seventy men's physical conditioning, including all the Officers".

In October 1989, at the age of 25 he joined the Marines. After billeting at Lympstone CTCRM and then at Norton Manor Camp, Andy bought a house in 1993 in Creech St. Michael, a small, peaceful village, east of Taunton. He moved several times buying properties in and around Taunton. And Taunton has been his home ever since.

During one of the regular nights ashore in Taunton Andy met his future wife Suzanne Rice. They married in 1998 and in 2005, Jacob Alexander was born. Sadly, Andy and Suzanne have subsequently divorced.

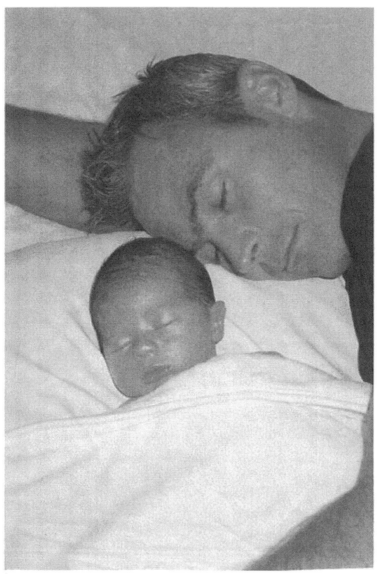

Andy with baby Jacob, just out of Intensive Care

Like Son!

Like Father

In the course of his time in the Marines, Andy qualified as

Andy at Lympstone CTC

a coach in a number of sports and he qualified as a skilled computer maintenance and repair technician as part of his resettlement. Without any relevant experience, such is his strength of character and determination he continued to push himself and the list of Instructor Certificate awards is quite remarkable. In no particular order, here are Andy's certificates...

- Registered Instructor & Teacher Advanced Level 3: Personal Trainer, Gym and Circuits

- British Weight-Lifters Association Instructors Award
- St John Ambulance First Aid
- ECB Coaching Level 2
- ECB Coaching Level 3
- ECB Coaching Level 4
- SAQ training (Speed, Agility & Quickness) where Andy passed with an effective pass mark of 112%; some achievement.
- Badminton Leaders Certificate
- Volleyball and Basketball coaching certificates.

Whilst still in the Marines Andy was awarded a coaching certificate from the Football Association and another certificate on the treatment and management of football injuries.

---oOo---

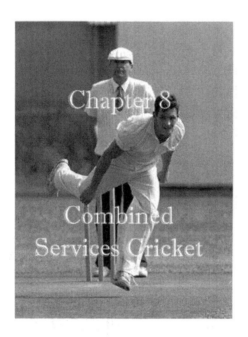

Back Row: Cpl N Palmer (Army Cpl A Jones (RAF) Lt A Falconer (RN) SAC M Turner (RAF) Cpl MD King (RM) Lt CA Slocombe (RN) LCpl A Hurry (RM)
Front row: Lt I Fielding (Army) Capt. RE Hollington (RM) Fl Lt AWJ Spiller (RAF) (Captain). Lt RJ Greaterex (Army) Capt. JWS Cotterill (Army)

Photograph reproduced courtesy of Owen Munford Studios

Chapter 8

Combined Services Cricket

Andy's entry in the Cricket Archive Player Oracle, [1] begins on the 8th August 1983, in the fifty-four over Hilda Overy Trophy, with Andy playing for Suffolk Colts, at Queen's College Ground, Cambridge, batting at number five. He scored nineteen before being stumped by the wicketkeeper Coulman off the slow left-arm orthodox bowling of John Andrew Afford. He then bowled 7 overs, 2 maidens for 24 runs. Suffolk Colts lost the match.

Andy's next recorded match was playing for the National Association of Young Cricketers South against the National Association of Young Cricketers North . at Trafalgar Road, Southport on Tuesday 30th August 1983. The National Association of Young Cricketers, which is organised and run by MCC at Lord's has been in existence since 1964 and can claim credit for the beginning of the careers of many talented county and international cricketers.

Some of the more notable names are:

• Ray East   Essex

• Angus Fraser   Middlesex (played in the same team as Andy in 1983)

- Bob Woolmer   Warwickshire

- Mike Gatting   Middlesex

- Alistair Hignell   Gloucestershire
- Mark Simmons   Durham

- Phil Neale   Worcestershire

- Graeme 'Foxy' Fowler Lancashire and Durham

And so, the list goes on…………….

In that fixture for the NAYC up in Southport, I had the privilege of rooming with a future England great, Angus Fraser. Gus and I opened the bowling together and I became aware very on in that game, that I had a long way to develop to get to his level. He consistently hit awkward areas and hit the pitch harder than me. He was so quiet in the evenings, but I couldn't have wished for a better roomie. Now we lock horns as Directors of Cricket but it is always great to spend some time with him, he is a great man.

On the 11th July 1991 Andy played for the Royal Navy in a fifty-five over match at Imber Court, East Molesey, which is a stone's throw from Hampton Court, and is the home ground of the British Police. The Navy lost the match but Andy played admirably, with figures of 11 overs, 1 maiden and 1 wicket for 59 runs. He also carried his bat with 21 runs. Playing alongside Andy was his good friend Chris Slocombe, who was a pilot with 846 Naval Air Squadron.

Andy played for the Combined Services, well known as being the breeding ground for several successful cricketers; for example, Fred Trueman, Brian Close, Jim Parks and Fred Titmus as well as the man himself, Andy Hurry.

Andy's cricketing brain developed and improved during his time in the Marines and this, coupled with his uncanny ability of spotting the strengths and weaknesses in his fellow players and his talent of helping them to attenuate their weaknesses and build on their strengths, became a powerful motivator for him.

In the author's opinion Andy has the same mind-set and commands the same respect and loyalty as other great sporting captains and managers;

All these managers rely upon the players under their guidance for success but there is, of course, a mutual relationship between them.

The gulf between a good leader and a truly great leader is vast and is, I contest, in most cases, unbridgeable and people ask the question; "Is a true leader made or born"?

That's a difficult one; Psychology textbooks answer that question so; *"The job of leading an organisation, a military unit, or a nation, and doing so effectively, is fantastically complex. To expect that a person would be born with all the tools needed to lead just doesn't make sense based on what we know about the complexity of social groups and processes"*

Leaders can indeed be developed. Yet, there is some "raw material," some inborn characteristics, that predispose people to be and to become leaders. These include but are not limited to:

- Extraversion, a term coined by the psychologist Jung, which means not being overly concerned with oneself or one's ego; The Oxford English Thesaurus defines extraversion as the quality of being outgoing and socially confident.
- Assertiveness
- Not afraid to take risks
- Intelligence
- Empathy

Andy has these characteristics in bundles; indeed, when Andy was spotted by Kevin Shine in the indoor nets, giving one-to-one coaching to a batter, Kevin remarked that he hadn't ever seen that amount of focus or one-to one dedication like that before and it had a profound effect on him.

---o0o---

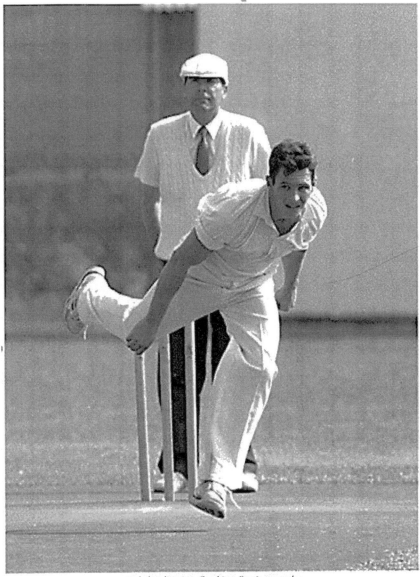

Andy bowling in a Combines Services match

Andy, in full swing, lofting one over the long-on boundary

Chapter 9

Life after the
Royal Marines

Chapter 9

Life after the Royal Marines

On the 30th October 1989, Andy entered Lympstone CTC to begin training. And was discharged on the 10th March 1999, unsurprisingly, with an exemplary character reference.

Andy's photograph on joining the Royal Marines

Andy's discharge Certificate March 1999

At Andy's request, his career in the Royal Marines will not be discussed in detail in this book.

Having submitted his resignation letter, Andy was now in the final eighteen months in the Royal Marines. He had married a local girl, Suzanne Rice in 1998. They had a mortgage, were happy, settled and Andy was contemplating life outside of the Royal Marines. While he was still at Norton Manor Camp, Section Leader Andy Hurry enrolled onto an advanced Computer Maintenance and repair course.

He had to request entry to this course, as at the time (in 1997) the Navy or indeed any of the other services did not offer any formal training courses or resettlement for personnel leaving the service.

The Ministry of Defence publish a document entitled; *Career Transition Partnership quarterly statistics: UK Regular Service Personnel Employment Outcomes 2009/10 to 2013/14 Q1*, which states the following;

The *Career Transition Partnership* (CTP) began in 1998 and is a contractual arrangement between the Ministry of Defence and a contractor (Right Management) for delivering a resettlement package to eligible Service personnel. CTP provides employment support for personnel up to two years before and two years after leaving the Armed Forces'. It appears that because Andy had submitted his resignation in 1997, one year prior to its enactment, he would not have been eligible for the benefits of CTP. He did, however, receive some assistance from the Royal Marines during his transition.

Nevertheless, Andy finally left the Marines on the 10th of March 1999 and started looking for gainful employment within and further out in the confines of Taunton Deane.

"I received my final salary on the day that I was discharged from the Marines", Andy explains; "I'd already applied for several jobs but notwithstanding my skills and qualifications, I was knocked back and one of the excuses I was given was that ex-servicemen came with too much baggage, they were too regimented in their ways and not flexible enough".

This hurt and annoyed Andy a lot but he was unable to change people's mind as to this fallacy.

That this misconception exists is quite unfortunate but this book is not the right place to discuss this inequity.

Andy was recently married, had a mortgage and was living in Taunton with his then-wife Suzanne, who was working as a travel agent and as time went on, as Andy continued to search for a job, she became the main breadwinner.

Chapter 54, Paragraph 5453 in the Royal Navy. Responsive: Terminal Leave, states that; 'Terminal leave is granted so that, entitled personnel may use their last weeks in the Service to seek employment and make appropriate domestic arrangements.

He started his leave, confident that his skills and experience would reward him with a worthwhile career once he discharged from the Marines. Andy recalls that 5 weeks into his leave of absence, he still had not secured a job and he was starting to panic and was becoming somewhat disconsolate. Andy is a proud man; he had never been in this position before and he found it extremely frustrating. He sent a countless number of job applications and got just two interviews!

Andy continues the story; "so I'm just looking through all my documentation thinking, maybe I can fall back on the football or cricket coaching."

Then whilst looking through his certificates it struck him! The County

Ground is just down the road, let's go and have a word with them. "So, I went to the cricket board; they run all recreational cricket and county age group cricket. I met a gentleman called Andrew Moulding. Andrew was the Cricket Development Manager for the Somerset Cricket

Andrew Moulding   *Julian Wyatt*

Board and reporting to him were two guys, Julian Wyatt and Pete Anderson".

So, Andy arranged to meet Andrew Moulding and detailed his credentials to him; an ex-Royal Marine and PTI, with ECB Cricket Coaching badges to level 2, did they have any vacancies, perhaps coaching colts or schools' cricket? Unfortunately, Andrew said that they didn't have any opportunities but he took Andy's details and said he would be in touch if anything turned up. Another knock-back, another disappointment…and it was getting ever closer to Andy's final discharge date and last pay packet.

However, Andy's never-say-die approach kicked in and he made the decision to try The Somerset Cricket Board again but this time he'd try a different tack. Ten more days passed without a job interview or opportunity so he made his way down to the County Ground again to see Andrew Moulding with his new proposal.

"Look, I'm prepared to work for nothing", Andy said to Andrew; "I just need to get some experience". Andrew was obviously impressed with Andy's tenacity so he invited him in and asked him, initially to assist the other coaches. He started on a Monday and as happens with everybody he meets and interacts with; he made an immediate good impression. "On the Wednesday Andrew asked me to meet him in the office and offered me the opportunity to go out into the community with Piran Holloway, a coach, who, in line with professional cricketers at the time, had to find his own employment in the close season".

Vic Marks the well-respected Somerset and England all-rounder from Middle Chinnock, a village in-between

Crewkerne and Yeovil, tells the author that in 1999 many cricketers who may have had multi-year contracts with their clubs had to find work outside of the season. He tells a story about one Somerset player who spent his close season as a gravedigger!

The Essex fast bowler Derek Pringle, writing in the Cricket Paper, elaborates on this point; '*Harry Pilling, Lancashire's diminutive batsman and a dynamic fielder, occasionally spent his winter months as a grave digger, but then expectations were not as great then even for winners of the Gillette Cup...David Lloyd, now the doyen of Sky's commentary team, worked for a brewery selling beer.*

Vic Marks

Many others, including Vic, went out as overseas players to South Africa, Australia and New Zealand.

Matthew Engel of The Guardian, wrote of Vic, that; '.... everyone liked him and opponents respected him as well as liked him and he was a highly successful overseas pro in Western Australia; cricket's nicest man surviving in its toughest school. He is an even higher-class journalist and broadcaster: witty, shrewd and kindly....'. The author would happily spend time talking with and listening to Vic reminisce and share fascinating stories about other great players in the game and hear his dulcet tones as we so often do when listening to him in conversation with Jonathan Agnew on Test Match Special.

Piran Holloway, currently living in Australia. Co-Founder of Airbuilding

Andrew paired Andy with Piran Holloway, a Somerset batter and a coach in the community and the club's highest scorer in the 1999 season.

Piran would go out to schools during the day, then organise and run one to-one coaching sessions in the evenings. He'd let it be known that he wanted to cut back on his commitments and Andy coming in had given the Board the ideal opportunity to help him and they asked Andy to take over the schools that Piran was currently coaching.

Andy takes up the story; "….so I spent a week travelling around with him and we went to all the schools where he did the coaching. On a Monday, we'd have a session at lunchtime and one later in the afternoon. We would then come back to the ground and do some one-to-one coaching in the evening. That happened every day of the week in schools in Somerset, Dorset and Devon".

Andy continued; "…. they offered me all the schools that Piran had coached at; I knew where all the schools were, I'd met all the teachers and I was really comfortable with it. On a Tuesday and a Thursday evening, I could do some

Indoor coaching Somerset Cricket Board

one-to-one coaching in the indoor school from six to nine in the evening. That was working one-to-one with private clients who paid to have their sons coached and on a Friday night every other week I used to work with the county age groups assisting Pete Anderson and Julian Wyatt. This was an invaluable experience and very soon after that I was offered the under twelves Head Coach Position. I was given the freedom to build up my clientele so I decided to go self-employed and set up my own coaching business.

That was a very steep learning curve for me; I had to teach myself bookkeeping, tax returns, remember to pay my National Insurance stamp and perhaps most importantly, I needed a decent car, which I could rely on.... because without one I could not fulfil my job. I also needed to build up my reputation and my clients' trust".

Many of the schools, which Andy coached at didn't have a teacher specialising in sport and consequently didn't play much sport. He believed he had spotted an opportunity so he arranged to meet the head teachers in each of the schools, at which he coached - and at various other schools within his area of responsibility. If he were to make a success of this opportunity, he had to widen his appeal so Andy explained to all the heads, that as well as holding level 2 cricket coaching badges, he was also an FA qualified coach.

Some of the heads said that they were interested that Andy was able to offer this as well as the cricket and welcomed this approach....and as it does with schools' bush telegraph, word soon spread.

Andy picks up the story; "So, with some of them I just did football, some of them I did cricket in the summer and football in the winter. I'd find myself working in so many different environments, whether it be a field, like we've got out here at the county ground with loads of space", as we look out of the doors onto the field with the Marcus Trescothick stand opposite, "or working in a room this big with 15 kids".

Andy's office is not compact as such but it is as large as it needs to be and it is served by a spacious balcony extending along the width of the Andy Caddick Pavilion. He picks up the story again; "I had to be adaptable, I had to find a way to make sure the kids enjoyed themselves and that they had the opportunity to develop. That stretched me massively and it would have been ideal if I had that facility out there and I could rely on the weather…", as he looks out onto pitch outside his double doors, "…but literally if it was pouring down with rain - well I couldn't cancel the sessions because I would lose the money. I was only paid for the sessions that I did so I had to be creative and sometimes do sessions in tiny little spaces".

"As I say that really stretched my capabilities as a coach or a teacher or whatever you want to call it and all this alongside working the one-to-ones not only on a Tuesday and a Thursday, but also on a Saturday enabled me to make a reasonable living".

"On a Saturday I could work from ten in the morning to six at night; there'd be different age groups coming in in odd sessions for a couple of hours in the morning and we'd run two blocks of sessions. So Jack Leach would have been one of the boys that I worked with, coming in as a nine year old kid and I would have him from nine to eleven and then we'd have an older age group from eleven to one; we'd have fifteen minutes for lunch and then we'd do some more one-to-one coaching right the way through to 6:00 on a Saturday night".

Watching Andy as he talks about this episode in his life, one can see that the enthusiasm is still there; his eyes sparkle and he becomes quite animated. He's a firm believer in the adage; 'catch them young and they will be yours forever', or as William Wordsworth wrote in his poem, "My Heart Leaps Up" in 1802; *The Child is the father of Man*".

It's obvious that this period in his life holds many happy memories for Andy. He continues; "then in the summer, it was hard because all the schools broke up. So, what I used to do then was get heavily involved in the Somerset age groups and they have quite a good competitive programme. I would get a daily rate and a mileage allowance. All in all, I'd started to put together quite a nice little earner. I should put into context that it's nearly 20 years ago but I was self-employed and earning about £25,000", which is probably equivalent to £40,000 today.

Andy had started his coaching in April 1999 and it continued through to March 2001 and one afternoon towards the end of January 2001, his life was about to change forever.

Kevin Shine   *Peter Bowler*

Kevin Shine, the first team coach in 2001 takes up the story. "I'd been playing professional cricket for ten years, first with Hampshire, then Middlesex and I'd been at Somerset for three seasons, from 1996. But I decided to retire from playing at the end of the 1998 season and in 2001 I'd taken up the role at Somerset as first team coach.

One particular evening in January 2001 in the indoor school, Andy was coaching in one of the nets and I was working with Peter Bowler in an adjacent net. Apart from the sound of the ball echoing off the bat and the two conversations it was pretty quiet and I couldn't help listening to this guy in the nets next to me and thinking this guy's different.

He had a way about him that was compelling to listen to and I could see that the player he was coaching was making real progress. At this particular time Andy was working under the auspices of the Cricket Board with Andrew Moulding". Kevin continues; "It just happens that I had been trying to get hold of a proper strength and conditioning coach for a while because we were lacking that skill and expertise, as such at the club. So the next morning I went and spoke to Peter Anderson, the CEO at the time and basically said I've just seen this guy coaching one-to-one cricket and he's excellent; he's got the skills and attitude I think the club needs and he shows all the attributes of a good strength and conditioning coach, can I have him?

Peter was an extremely astute person and manager, with an enormous number of friends of influence and he asked me to leave it with him and he would get back to me."
Peter Anderson, or Panda to his friends has a long association with Somerset and was a pivotal influence in getting Viv Richards to sign for the club. Peter tells the story; "In 1973 I toured Antigua as part of my old friend and former Somerset chairman Len Creed's touring party". What happened then would prove crucial to the history of the Somerset County side – a chance to play against a young Viv Richards. Peter continues; "There were a few pros travelling with us, including Derek Underwood of Kent and Allan Jones of Glamorgan. Antigua batted first and got a big score and I bowled to Viv and managed to get him out for 20-odd, and believe me, I have never let him forget it"!

"I opened the batting with Jones and faced up to a young Andy Roberts...he was peppering me with short deliveries at devastating pace! I took one to the chest which knocked me over. The bruise was massive but I got a few runs that day, maybe 60-odd?"

Despite Viv's modest score, Bath bookmaker Creed signed the young Richards for his local club, Lansdowne CC, for the 1973 season, and it was during this time that Somerset saw him play and offered him a contract for 1974 and the rest, as they say, is history.

In the 1970's Peter played at Tavistock Cricket Club, along with Bill Alley, the Somerset and England player and later an international umpire.

Gerry Woodcock, in his book, *History of Tavistock Cricket Club 18491999: 150 Years of Cricket at the Ring [ISBN 978-0746309353]* relates a story about Peter, during his time at Tavistock Cricket Club; "....an amusing tale that caused a bit of a stink at the time was when in 1975 police inspector Peter Anderson was team captain he wanted to avoid problems with ponies galloping across the square. He was advised that tiger manure from Plymouth Zoo was the answer. It certainly kept the ponies away but also burnt the grass on the square and this took a long time to recover!

Kevin continues; "Peter was an ex-copper from Devon who was sent out to Hong Kong to deal with the corruption in the police force out there. He knew everybody and had some fantastic contacts". Peter came back next morning and said; "he's exactly who he says he is, you can have him for 3 or 4 mornings a week".

However, several weeks passed before Andy was offered a position by the club and he continued with his own coaching regime. To help him through the lean times he sought out other work and for a while was employed as a cleaner at Somerset College of Arts and Technology (SCAT) along the Wellington Road.

Andy continues; "…and then I got a phone call from Shiny a few weeks, maybe five weeks later, saying I'm interested in potentially you delivering some preseason fitness work for the pros, would you be interested in doing that"? "I said, yeah, I'd love to but it's got to fit around my self-employed work. I worked from something like, eight in the morning to half past eleven and then I'd go and do my school work and now I'm combining both and being paid for it and that went really well. I did the three weeks pre-season training and Shiny said he was really pleased at how that went and he'd had some good positive feedback from the players. On the back of this, still in 2001 they offered me an opportunity where I could still do my self-employed coaching and work from eight in the morning to eleven thirty on their fitness with the pros who may not have been picked or guys who were coming back from injury".

Kevin continues; "So Sarge did some coaching in the indoor school and came in and did some pre-season preparation for the guys in the morning and helped me by putting training programmes together. He also had a natural talent for analysing a player and quickly identifying his or her strengths and weaknesses and working to improve on the strengths, and challenging him to minimise their weaknesses"

"I very soon realised that I wanted this guy full time because there was more to him than a strength and conditioning coach because he had such a good cricket brain.

I had a triple whammy

1. An extremely good analyst

2. An excellent Strength and Conditioning coach and

3. A really keen cricket brain

©Midweek Herald   *Peter Anderson at Seaton Cricket Club*

Kevin again; "I used to love talking to him about what he was seeing and he quickly became my confidante. We travelled to every away game together. Nowadays teams travel to away matches in luxury coaches but back then players would have to make their own way to matches in their cars.

We worked very closely together on the plans that we thought would suit our players and he would always give me an honest opinion of what he was seeing with the players".

"The more that he did the more that you could see that he was growing within the game and I would say that as a man, he was beyond reproach! Nothing was too much trouble for him; ask him to do a job and it would be done accurately and diligently and if he wasn't ever sure, he would never assume but always ask for clarification".

Kevin continues; "He is one of the most remarkable characters I've ever had the pleasure to know; the way he looked after himself, his self-discipline" ......he recounts an example......" We used to do a canal run; the boys didn't really like to do it but Sarge knew that there was only one way to get the boys' total input, trust and enthusiasm.

Once on the canal tow path he was always the first up to the turn round point *and first back every time* to encourage the players on and make sure everybody came back, were all OK and there weren't any injuries. They may not have enjoyed it but whatever Sarge asked them to do the players did it unflinchingly and with a smile. He has always led from the front; he is a born leader.

He is diligent, hardworking and conscientious and his analyses were meticulous and were full of little insights and astute observations. It was great watching him; he would put cameras in odd places, up flagpoles or light stands for example so that he could get several different views for his analysis. He'd sit with the players and discuss the analysis and he always asked them what they thought and very often included their input in his submissions to me.

He would finish his analyses and then just come down and continue with the coaching and he has this uncanny ability to be able to focus on one person without it being detrimental to the rest of the team. The boys loved it and they loved him and they benefitted enormously from him. He built and encouraged a real tight team spirit. They all looked out for each other and became extremely close as a unit. He did the analysis for three years and in that time, we became ever closer professionally and personally. Wonderful times!

He was massively, massively confident and really well-liked by everybody.

He was such a valuable member of the team. He just grew as a coach and became an integral part of the team.

---oOo---

Peter Trego and I are sitting in the Weston-Super-Mare box overlooking the pitch and watching the ground staff cutting the grass. He had just deputised for Tom Abell as captain and it is obvious, he is Somerset through and through and he tells me it is a huge honour to; "…lead the boys out…." He articulates well and doesn't feel the need to pepper his conversation with clichés. I remind him that he was adjudged the leading all-rounder in county cricket in 2007. He tells me that it was a privilege and an honour to play for the club when Brian Rose was the Director of Cricket and Justin Langer was captain and Andy was the coach.

I then asked him; "I know when we did the press conference and you were saying that when you knew Sarge was coming back, everybody was really pleased and I presume yourself, you are very pleased about that as well because of the influence he may have had on you; we are talking of 12 years ago, aren't we"? "One hundred percent", Peter responds, "Yeah, it's a long time, although it doesn't feel long. And I think the one thing that I suppose shows what the club means to Sarge and Sarge means to the club is even during his time away he still was around and you always felt that he had a great interest in what we're all doing. I think I sponsored him a few times for a few of the charity runs that he was doing and so I'm always in touch with him. But I think part of the reason why I think we're doing so well is - a club like Somerset is massively built on relationships and I think even though we're a very big club in terms of how good we are as a team, there's still that, well, sort of small club mentality. But I mean that in the good sense of the words; when Sarge announced he was coming back, people like myself, James Hildreth and Tres (Marcus Trescothick) the......sort of older spine of the squad if you like, had immensely fond memories of a great period in Somerset history under Sarge and Justin Langer [In 2006 – 2007]. So that was a great time, a great feeling but also with Jason Kerr dovetailing as Head Coach with Sarge as Director of cricket, virtually every young player that we've got has come through Jason's time with the academy. When you look at each individual and their relationships with their seniors, there's really strong personal friendships and associations there and that I think has a lot to do with how well we gel as a team...."

Peter stresses the next point; "… and never undervalue [the power of] trust in a sports environment, especially the trust that's been built over a great many years here at the club even though this management group is new". Trust is a byword in the vocabulary of so many of the Somerset staff, players and administrators. I tell him; "Well, I'll tell you what, what, what you've just said there is mirrored by Spencer Bishop, Ben Warren by Andy and by Jason Kerr". Peter jokes; "well they just stole my words. What can

I say? I told them that they just keep copying me". Laughing, I interject; "but the thing is, all joking aside, it is really impressive that even in adversity when perhaps you're not doing so well, that you can still see that the ethos around the club is strong enough to actually keep people together and keep everybody's heads up because it would be so easy for the heads to drop, wouldn't it"?

Peter again; "Yeah, of course. We've got a training day today. We're about to travel to Chelmsford to face Essex, which is an exceptionally long journey on the team coach. I came in four hours early today. The physio department was full, with the majority of the squad sat in front of the television, watching Dom Bess playing for England [England vs Pakistan] and getting his cap from Vic [Marks]. A number of players and coaching staff joined me in the gym, talking over what we needed to do to keep ourselves fit and I think in a non-functioning game environment that wouldn't happen; people would be watching at home on their own. So even when we don't have to be here, we're drawn to the club - drawn to each other, which is a really strong thing. Peter is a striking individual, jet-black hair, head shaved on both sides and the oiled hair on top swept back.

Peter Trego scoring a four to the point boundary

I comment about his impressive tan and he points out that he's been told he has 'Red Indian' blood; I take him at his word. As with the rest of the team, he takes his training seriously and says that the credit for that rests squarely with Andy.

James Hildreth

So back to 2001 and Andy now employed by Somerset as a Strength and Conditioning coach and analyst. Andy says that those three years working with Shiny [Kevin Shine] hold some of his fondest memories. He experienced the camaraderie of the dressing room and lived the ups-and downs of each individual player's day-to-day moods. Andy compares the dressing room at a professional cricket club to a barracks in the Royal Marines, where the Marine Troop live as a family unit, with some individuals getting closer to their colleagues than with their own family. Without going into too much detail about the structure of the Commando Troop, suffice to say that it is important that the person who would be required to lead a section of four to eight men should have a strong character or certain characteristics that make him stand out from and lead his peers in times of stress. It may be that the person who is selected to lead the team has within him the strength of character to lift his colleagues' spirits when the going gets tough….as it ultimately does, whether training or on the front line is gruelling. In other words, it is vital to maintain a sense of humour. We all recognise that humour is therapeutic; as Psychology Today argues; "…. having a sense of humour about life's difficulties can provide a way to bond with others, look at things in a different way, normalise your experience and keep things from appearing too overwhelming or scary. Properly developed, a good sense of humour can keep people and relationships strong".

Andy compares Peter Trego to the team leader because he considers that he has the strength of character to lift his team-mates when the going gets tough. Peter is surprised and delighted at the same time. He says that for him at least, things started to change when Andy arrived and later when Justin was captain.

That is very much in the future though because at present in this chronology Andy has achieved ECB Performance Coaching Level 1 and 2 through the Combined Services. In order for him to progress to formally coaching a County Cricket team, he would need his ECB Performance Coaching Levels 3 and 4.

Although Andy was at this time, still under the jurisdiction of the Somerset Cricket Board, Kevin Shine and Somerset Cricket Club were suitably impressed with Andy's cricket knowledge, self-discipline and the respect, with which he was held by all he interacted with and the obvious ambitions he harboured for the game, so much so that Kevin recommended Andy should apply to study for his Level 3 Elite Coach Development Programme. Andy was keen to apply for it but without the Cricket Club acting as Sponsor for his application, he wouldn't have been accepted onto the programme. In order for Andy to progress as a coach, he would have to 'get his' Level 3 and Level 4 performance coaching badges. The ECB writes on their website that; *'Coaches interested in attending the ECB performance coach course will be required to hold an existing Level 2 qualification or equivalent, have acquired some experience of working with the most talented young players, and demonstrate a willingness and open-mindedness to learn'.*

So, Kevin arranged for him to study to pass both courses, saying; "It is extremely rare for a non-player to reach the heights that Andy has and he has done it brilliantly."

In order to attract enough applicants and ensure that they covered the whole country, the ECB organised regional Elite Coach Development courses. Coincidentally the next Level Three Performance Coach Course was to be conducted in the South West at Taunton. In the autumn of 1999, he was enrolled onto the course, under the direction of Gordon Lord.

The course, at the time, was flexible and allowed Andy to continue his work for the Cricket Board and also to continue his self-employment. So, over a period of several weekends and much hard work, he passed and in his own words; "…. honestly, it went really well…"

After retiring from professional cricket Gordon Lord took up the role of Senior Coach Development Manager at the ECB.

He was presented with the certificate by Gordon on the 7th Nov 1999. During the course Andy forged a close friendship with Gordon, a friendship, which has continued to this day and this trust and friendship would open up new and seemingly unobtainable avenues for Andy; more of which will be discussed later in the book.

Kevin continues; "I'm not surprised to see how far he has gone now and to be back at Somerset. I have a huge place in my heart for Somerset and for him. I trusted Andy implicitly when I was Head Coach and he never let me

Gordon Lord

down once. I am proud that I have played a small part in where Andy is now. I count him as a true friend. He still has ambitions and it would not surprise me to see him as England Coach one day. Worthy praise indeed.

Andy & Amy at the end of season dinner 2018 (Andy's 1ˢᵗ Year as DOC)

Pete, Bethany, Mimi and Jacob in the Family Enclosure at Lord's for the
RLODC Final

A young Jacob on holiday

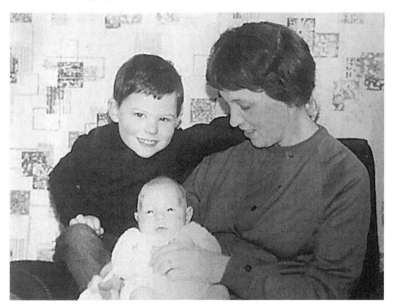

Peter's christening 1968. Andy, Mum & Peter.

Jacob with Helen at Edinburgh castle on her 80th birthday

Andy, Helen and John on their 1st holiday in Swansea

*Jacob proudly wearing a
Baggy Green at the Oval*

*Jacob & Justin Langer Cricket World Cup match Australia vs
Pakistan 2019*

*Peter & Andrew after the Royal London One Day
Cup Final*

*Tom Lammonby from SCCC Academy signing a
professional Contract at Exeter CCC*

14Amy, Poppy, Mimi and Jacob on our first holiday together in 2010

Chapter 11

Chapter 11
Taunton and the Cooper
Associates County Ground

Chapter 11

Taunton and the Cooper Associates County Ground

Taunton, the county town of Somerset, sits between the Quantock, Blackdown and Brendon hills in an area known as the Vale of Taunton. As well as being home to 40 Commando at Norton Manor Camp since 1983, Taunton is home to an abundance of successful sports clubs and organisations, which cater for all ages.

The various clubs offer both able-bodied and physically impaired Korfball[1], Fencing, Angling, Tennis, Badminton, Football, American Football, Baseball, Equestrian Sports, Weight-lifting, Swimming, Bowls, Rowing, Cricket and many, many more.

Taunton Racecourse, which hosts National Hunt Racing is situated 2 miles south of Taunton in Orchard Portman.

Somerset County Cricket Club have their headquarters and play their home matches at The Cooper Associates County Ground in Taunton.

It is in many people's opinion one of the most attractive and definitely family-friendly cricket grounds in the country.

Nestling just on the edge of the town centre and adjacent to the River Tone, the ground is overlooked by the impressive bell tower of St James'

Anglican Church. In the near distance can be seen the spire of St. Mary's church. Both churches date back to the Tudor period and St. James' holds parish records dating back to 1610.

Situated just a stone's throw outside the Joel Garner Gates and on the same side of the river is the Brewhouse Theatre, Taunton's largest auditorium. On the opposite side of the river stands a large Morrison's supermarket and sited adjacent to the supermarket car park are the rear entrances to the several shops and businesses fronting onto Station Road.

The County Ground has entry 4 gates; they are the Sir Viv Richards Gate, the Jack White Gate, the Brian Rose Gate and the Joel Garner Gate.

Somerset is noted for its River end and the Pavilion End; up until 2015, a grand white wooden Pavilion, which had stood since 1881, dominated the Pavilion end. Discussions about renewing the old pavilion had been going on for several years but it was not until October 2013 that the

Somerset Committee submitted the final designs and planning permission was granted.

Old Pavilion   *Photos courtesy of Somerset Grockles*   New Pavilion

Scyld Berry, the Telegraph Cricket Correspondent, asked the question;

"Where is the best place to watch cricket"?

He answered his own question thus; "Not heaven. That must be an aerial view, and you want to be behind the arm. Not Adelaide Oval. The beautiful backdrop of the cathedral, and the century-old scoreboard and the Adelaide Hills, but the drawback lies in the name on the tin. It is an Oval, and if you are behind the arm the action is too far away.

Not Lord's either. An excellent view from either end, but if you are a member sitting in the pavilion you are in the shade, and if you are in the media centre you cannot hear

a sound. It is insulated, air-conditioned and remote from the game, like too many modern press boxes.

Edgbaston's new media centre is very good but a bit too high. Trent Bridge's is a bit too low, so the umpire can obscure the ball's flight. Old Trafford's is just about the right height, but again behind glass, which won't open.

No, the best place in the world to watch cricket has to be Taunton, in the Old Pavilion, right behind the arm". A real testament from a media giant!

The new pavilion is designed to try and emulate the atmosphere of the old wooden pavilion and the media centre is just the perfect place to watch the game, listen to the badinage and occasionally join in the witty banter. The day is punctuated with often clever and funny, pithy observations from Richard Walsh, a man, who like Scyld, knows the game and personalities of cricket 'inside out'.

Richard Walsh

In November 2015, Guy Lavender, the then CEO opened the new pavilion on the site of the old white painted wooden pavilion. Sitting in the media centre atop the new pavilion, one looks out at the Quantock Hills 17 miles in the distance. Tim Heald, in his book, 'The Character of Cricket' discusses a time when a vice president of the club, a structural engineer in Yeovil told him of an old adage, which was related to him by ...an old Aunt in Creech St. Michael; "If you can see the Quantocks, it means rain and if you can't it's raining already"!

The Quantocks form the backdrop to the lush greenery of the many deciduous trees surrounding the spire of St Andrew's Church. This landscape draws the eye back into the County Ground and to the impressive stock brick constructed Sir Ian Botham Stand, which is flanked on one side by the Marcus Trescothick stand and the Colin Atkinson stand on the other side.

---The Andy Caddick Pavilion---

Andy returned to Somerset in 2017 as Director of Cricket and he says; "….it felt like I was coming home but I know I have a big job to do…."

Former bowling coach and now Head Coach Jason Kerr, ably assists him. Jason is a straight-talking, pleasant and courteous Lancastrian who hails from Bolton.

Jason and Andy have an office on the top floor of the Andy Caddick Pavilion, which houses the gymnasium, the players' dining room and dressing room - and the indoor school.

Another person occupying the top floor is the Chief Operating Officer, Sally Donoghue, who in her 30 years with the club has held many different positions and her

Elton John concert at Somerset County Cricket Ground, 3rd June 2012

role now involves not only running the club but also organising other events in the close season.

She loves working at Somerset and she says of her happiest memories; "...the highlights would have to be winning the Twenty20 Cup in 2005; promotion back to Division I of the County Championship in 2007; my trip to India with the squad in 2009 for the Champions League and of course, hosting last year's England IT20.

"Some of my proudest moments have also been from hosting the large concerts on the outfield, [*Elton John and Rod Stewart to name but two*].

Our first one in 2006 [*Elton John*] was a massive learning curve for everyone. We were a small team who just rolled up their sleeves and got on with it and did it really well and continue to do so – we definitely punch above our weight! To be around professional sport is a great thing to be a part of and it's so refreshing. People are in and out all the time and the players are such fun to be around".

"There's nothing that beats the atmosphere when the players first go out onto the pitch and the crowd are all clapping and cheering."

The Ticket Office and Reception are on the ground floor of the Caddick stand. On entering the reception, Nicola Hockey and Val Baker greet everyone with a warm smile. One gains access to the main office complex through reception. Along with the other members of staff, Nicola and Val report to Sarah Trunks, a bright, intelligent 32-year-old from Watchet.

Her team comprises

- Head of Commercial Sales: Sam McIntyre
- Commercial Sales & Support Executive: Brian Lee
- Commercial Sales Executive: Bryn Jones
- Ticketing & Membership Executive: Nicola Hockey
- Customer Service Executive: Val Baker
- Media & Community Executive: Spencer Bishop

- Digital Marketing & Communications Executive: Ben Warren
- Sarah has been with Somerset for 9 years and she has worked her way up the career ladder, beginning as a receptionist.

Very often one would climb the stairs to Andy's office and see the players' lobby chock full of cricket bags and 'coffins' and watch the players in the indoor school or exercising in the gym.

Also located in the Andy Caddick Pavilion is the Somerset Cricket Board, created in 1994 and the Board, also has its offices in the indoor school.

---o0o---

Chapter 11

Triumvirate

Chapter 11

Triumvirate

Andy Hurry readily admits that following the disastrous 2006 season the club needed a rethink. Justin Langer (Alf), Andy Caddick and Marcus were instrumental in helping turn the fortunes of the club around in their valuable contributions in formulating a strategy. The input of players like Marcus, Caddy and Alf on the field and, as importantly in the dressing room was key and Andy recalls; "The young players and the less experienced players bought in to the leadership and trusted the leaders' decision-making processes and whatever the decision was, everyone believed in it and we went with it and that worked really successfully."

If 2006 was the nadir, then there was only one way to go…... Andy was fortunate that he had Brian Rose, one of the game's great thinkers as his Director of Cricket and Richard Gould as the Chief Executive. That was a powerful combination, Andy, Richard and Brian.

Richard Gould, the son of legendary West Ham footballer Bobby Gould is the embodiment of a confident self-assured leader and, as is common with people who 'know themselves, 'he is self-effacing and understands completely the philosophy and importance of a team - but as a former Tank Commander, Richard also understands the loneliness of being a 'Captain of Industry'.

Richard finished his 'A' Levels at Bristol Grammar School and entered The Royal Military Academy (RMA) at Sandhurst, following which, he was commissioned into the Royal Tank Regiment as a tank Commander. When asked what appealed to him about the Tank Regiment, Richard responded with straight-faced wit; "I looked at the infantry and they have to walk everywhere and I thought, well, at least with the tank regiment you get a ride!"

Richard continues; "Giles Clark, who was chairman at the time, invited me down here from Bristol City, where I had been Commercial Director for 6 years with Colin Sextone. Andy Nash had joined the board the year previously, so we had a lot of experience". Richard replaced Peter Anderson, who had been at the helm since 1989. Brian Rose also joined at about the same time, as Director of Cricket, which Richard recalls; "to me was an absolute delight". 2005 saw the club in a period of transition and Rosey (Brian Rose) knew what needed to be done on the field and I knew what needed to be done off the field because having been at City, which is a well-developed commercial club there were lots of 'low hanging fruit'", which as we shall see later in this chapter is another example of Richard's euphemistic nature. One of the factors, which Richard says helped to put the club back on a 'proper footing' was Rosey recruiting Andy Hurry.

He continues; "The board had discussed the availability of several coaches but it has to be said that Brian knew exactly what and who he wanted. Andy had worked at the club a few years before, looking after the 'juniors' and I think Brian had been so impressed by his organisation and his leadership skills that despite Andy never having played at County Level Cricket, he was a very, very good cricketer with the Combined Services, Brian thought that he was exactly the right character to come in and work with him". "One of my observations, when I came from football and into cricket, was that in football, you know who's in charge of playing staff, namely the manager.

In cricket, I've always found it a little bit less clear cut. Who picks the team? Is it the coach, the captain, the director of cricket, chairman of selectors or the chairman?"

"We decided that we wanted to set up a more 'transparent' system, where people knew exactly what their role was. So, having brought in Andy Hurry as Head Coach and Justin Langer as captain we had what I called the cricket triumvirate and they formed a very strong and successful team".

Author's note: [*Andy has specifically stated that team selection is not part of his role; that responsibility lies entirely with Jason Kerr, the Head Coach.*]

Richard is reluctant to take credit for his part in the change in fortunes at Somerset, saying, quite blithely; "…. because I never take wickets. I don't score runs. I didn't have a great deal of day to day interaction with the players. My role was to help guide the management team effectively and if you've got a good team they just get on and do it. However, sometimes if you've got a slightly more objective view, perhaps, then they'll listen. I think the advantage that I've got is going back through my old man and his football days, because I remember when my old man was a manager and the feedback from him as to how he was being dealt with, by his board and his chief executives and sometimes when he was going through a really difficult patch, um, what he really needed more than anything was the supportive arm rather than a critical comment.

When Richard left Somerset in 2011, Andy Nash was generous in his praise saying; "I have mixed feelings in confirming that Richard Gould will be moving to Surrey to further his career. I'm absolutely delighted that he has secured such an excellent opportunity and it reflects very well on Somerset that we are developing not only our players for England but also our senior managers to go on to prestigious roles and greater challenges".

"I'm grateful to Surrey Chairman, Richard Thompson for the sensitive way in which the matter was handled - both clubs acted with great integrity. At the same time, I am very sorry to see Richard move on as he has been a truly great companion, colleague and combatant to work alongside". "Richard joined us in 2005 when the club's fortunes were at a low ebb. Since then he has played a leading role in driving forward the redevelopment of the

County Ground and the dramatic improvement in our financial position and prospects".

---oOo---

Brian Rose

Brian should have been born in Weston-Super-Mare, however, fate dictated that he be born in Kent, in Horton Kirby, 5 miles southeast of Dartford in 1950, as a result of his parents visiting his poorly grandfather in Swanley and Brian arriving earlier than expected.

Dartford is notable in that Margaret Roberts, soon to become Thatcher, lost two general elections in this safe Labour seat in 1950 and 1951.

Brian Rose & Tom Abell at Lord's 2019

In 1958 Brian's father was posted to Singapore and they stayed out there until 1962 when he was posted back to

Locking again; as Brian says with a straight face; "…..mainly because he was the wicket-keeper with Weston's cricket team and he'd also played with the Combined Services out in Singapore".

Brian Rose or 'Rosey' as he is known affectionately by his friends, began his career at Somerset in 1969, was captain of Somerset for six years from 1978 and he led the county to its first ever trophies, the Gillette Cup and the John Player League, in 1979. He ended his playing career in 1987 owing to chronic back problems and his diminishing sight. I caught up with Brian at his favourite restaurant in Weston-Super-Mare.

Renowned as one of the game's real thinkers, he was probably the ideal man to lead Somerset through its period of transition. During our conversation I asked him what his father did in the RAF; "…. basically, just played cricket and football", was his amusing response.

Born in Worcester, Rosey's father was a keen footballer who had had trials with West Bromwich Albion and he was a good enough left winger to have become a professional footballer had he not, at the age of 18, been called up for National Service, joined the RAF and been sent off to India and Burma.

The conversation returns to cricket; "…. I think one of my earliest memories as Director of Cricket (DOC) was when I was asked prior to my retirement in 2004 I think it was, to write a report on the current state of the cricket at Somerset. As a result of that report, in early August, I decided to travel up to the game at Chester-Le-Street. Ricky Ponting was over for about six weeks and I wanted to watch him play. (*The weather was atrocious for the Frizzell County Championship match, which started on Friday, August 13th and only one day's play was possible. The Totesport League Division two day-night match took place on the Wednesday prior. Somerset won the match by four wickets, albeit by the Duckworth Lewis method, a system, which recalculates target scores in rain-affected matches*). Ricky top scored on 83 not out and was the man-of-the-match. During my stay in Durham, I had several long sessions and discussions with him. I also took the opportunity to interview some of the players and several of the coaching staff to get a better understanding of who would continue to be an asset to the club and whom the club wanted to move on. Andy Hurry at the time was the strength and fitness coach so I also had a brief word with him.

Around about this time, Somerset CCC was going through the process of transition but the committee wasn't entirely certain about which way to go.

Brian continues; "I'd already helped write two or three reports for the ECB, one of which was the Schofield Report, published in May 2007 and I had submitted a report, which I'd written jointly with Roy Kerslake, to the Somerset Committee about the state of cricket at Somerset CCC.

I recall that it was recognised by almost everybody at the club that there was a very strong bond between Andy and the players in terms of his professionalism, his expectations, his manner, and his meticulous recordkeeping and intimate knowledge of the players and the game."

"I'd had discussions with the committee members and Giles Clark agreed with my recommendation, to appoint a Chief Executive Officer (CEO) and a DOC and I took on the role of DOC and Richard Gough was appointed to the position of CEO."

One of Brian's many strengths was in identifying exceptionally good young players and introducing them to the club. One of the most successful introductions was Marcus Trescothick.

Photograph courtesy of © Somerset CCC

In years past most cricket clubs toured around their counties as part of the summer festival. This allowed supporters in the outlying districts of the county to watch the club's first and second teams and they could appreciate the massive talents of Marcus or 'Tres' as he is known. Sadly, Somerset, along with most other counties has stopped this practice.

Staying on the topic of Tres, Brian recalls the following anecdote; "One of my earliest memories as DOC was when Mark Garaway was the coach in 2005. We'd already won the T20; I hadn't arrived until late May or early June but I'd recognised quite early on that we needed a few changes especially in terms of professionalism among the players and staff, meaning that he considered that there wasn't enough discipline in the team, either self or imposed".

"Following Tim Boon's departure from the England set-up, the ECB approached Mark Garaway to take up a role as an analyst. He told me quite early in the season that he was going to accept the role and that gave me quite a few months to appoint a new Head Coach, make some personal contacts and have some conversations with the players whom I knew I wanted to keep and see in which direction they thought the club should be going. I felt it was vital to get input from as wide a scope as possible. The committee agreed with me that it would be of benefit to the Head Coach if I retained complete control over the budget and the authority to hire and fire". More on this later on in the book.

"Had you seen Marcus play at Keynsham?" "Yes, I'd taken an interest in Marcus from when he was playing age group cricket at the age of 13 and I consider that even at that age you can see if a boy has a good eye. I always felt that I was able to identify talent at a young age. I was 'pretty successful' at hiring and firing and bringing young talent to the club. I'd brought Marcus into the club and I knew he was a prodigious talent but in 1996 he wasn't being played; this was really frustrating, so following the NatWest Bank Trophy Quarter-Final against Surrey at the Oval on the last day of July I dropped Andy Hayhurst, the captain and Vice-captain Peter Bowler took over."

The Independent newspaper wrote of this decision; 'Somerset yesterday showed how little room there was for sentiment in cricket when they dropped their captain, Andy Hayhurst, from the team to play Hampshire because they felt he was not playing well enough to justify keeping out younger players. Peter Bowler, the club's vice-captain, has taken charge of the team. Hayhurst, 33, has not been stripped of the captaincy, which he has held since 1994 but needs to improve his form in order to force his way back, says Brian Rose, the Somerset Chairman. Hayhurst has scored 224 runs in the Championship this

Andy Caddick

season at an average of 18. Hayhurst's replacement in the team, the 20-year-old Marcus Trescothick, scored 178 as Somerset ended the first day on 412 for 6'.

Brian continues; "It was wonderful to watch Marcus grow and to eventually get into the England side and become one of the greatest players this county and his country has produced". He continues; "we had several personality issues, which were starting to affect the character and attitude at the club around this time". Marcus and Caddy helped in this very much. "So, you used them as a sounding board"?

"Well yes, because of my strong relationship with Caddy and I'd brought Marcus into the club when I was Chairman of the club

"Back to 2006 and the poor end to the season that we'd all endured. Because of the invaluable input from the players and the support of the committee in agreeing to implement the various strategies we had discussed, I was much closer to achieving the professionalism in the side, for which I was looking. Andy Hurry fitted into this structure perfectly, bringing enormous energy, discipline, camaraderie and knowledge into the team. By the start of the 2007 season, the club, including me, were delighted that everything had fallen into place within a year because these plans and changes can sometimes take several years to mature…."

"….so, the plan was to have a coach like Andy to work with a strong, qualified captain. Although he probably wouldn't have admitted it at the time, Andy needed me to do the hiring and firing, which allowed him to concentrate his efforts on the cricket and taking the team forward, which by the end of the season, was a great success as we won promotion to the first division". Andy echoes Brian's contention regarding recruitment and retention of staff, saying; "Brian is 100 per cent correct; we could then focus on the cricket. Moreover, as I alluded to, it gave my team the freedom to operate how we wanted to, and you know, some of it can be very, very challenging as I am finding out now is that retaining and recruiting players is very demanding. It's quite a long process, it's not just one conversation; they tend to go on for a long time and sometimes you're waiting to make the next decision on the outcome of the previous conversation.

I ask; "is that because you're dealing with egos or because you're dealing with the agents or both"?

"It's a combination of everything, you know; the player's and the club's perceptions might be different. Dealing with agents…. well understandably, they are operating in the best interest of their client…. but that might not fit in with what we are looking for. Moreover, for someone like Brian to take that responsibility off my shoulders, just freed me up to really concentrate and focus on the cricket."

Brian remarks that; "...the atmosphere at Somerset was quite unique, particularly from the early '70s, with the signing of Tom Cartwright and Derek Taylor followed by Viv Richards and Peter Denning. Ian Botham starting to come through from the juniors and the classic signing of 'Big Bird' Joel Garner, meant that by the time I took over as captain we had a superlative team and fantastic support from the fans and the sponsors. The Sunday League for sell-out and you couldn't get a ticket love nor, the money. Wherever we went matches were a crowd were really friendly and it helped to boost the membership.

---oOo---

United Arab Emirates, the First Time

Chapter 12

United Arab Emirates the First Time

As has already been discussed in the book, in 2001, Andy resigned from coaching age group cricket with the Somerset Cricket Board and assumed the role of Strength & Fitness Coach with Somerset CCC, with CEO Peter Anderson.

Andy continued in this role and that of the assistant coach until 2005 when the club implemented the review about its operations, which the committee had been discussing. On implementation of said review, conducted by Brian Rose, Kevin Shine was moved from first team Head Coach to academy director, Mark Garraway moved from Academy director, second eleven coach to the first team Head Coach, and they offered Andy the opportunity to run the second eleven. Andy continues; "I'm quite a loyal person but I found myself in what I thought was a difficult position, where I didn't want to 'pin my flag' to any particular mast. To me, relationships are extremely important and it was something I personally found quite challenging..." I ask him what he found challenging and he continues; "…you imagine that the first team coach is now working as an academy coach and the academy second eleven coach is now working as first team coach. One of those 'guys' is happy about that, the other one's not so happy and I found the whole situation quite uncomfortable. Don't get me wrong, I was grateful for the opportunity to lead the second eleven but it wasn't sitting comfortably with me, how I found myself - in the middle of a situation that had a degree of bitterness; it questioned my loyalty."

"It got to the point where, one day in early spring, while I was at the local gym in town, I ran into an old colleague of mine from the Royal Marines. During our discussions, he said that he was going to the airport the next week to fly out to the UAE, to Dubai, to take up a role working for a civilian contract company with the United Arab Emirates armed forces. He would be instructing their military command personnel and upskilling them to move them toward the levels of the British armed forces and in particular, the standards of the Royal Marines. I felt that that was quite an exciting opportunity for him and he said if you ever fancy it, with your experience, you'd get a job out there any time you wanted to..."

United Arab Emirates, the First Time

"...and so, because I was feeling unsure about the environment here at the club, I thought to myself, well, that's a fantastic opportunity. The salary was very attractive. My colleague told me that the company looked after its employees well and I thought...well, it could be a new challenge for me... My thinking was that if I did it for 10 years, it could set me up for life. My wife Suzy and I could rent out our property in Taunton. All of our expenses were paid for out in the UAE so it was a bit of a no brainer really. My old colleague and I met up again and out of that meeting, they offered me an interview down in Exeter the next day. I attended the interview and the company offered me a job straight away so I went back to the club and handed in my notice and told them I was leaving." I ask Andy; "did the club ask you to reconsider your decision"?

"Yes, they tried to change my mind but I was determined; I'd made my mind up, having given it considerable thought. My thinking was that this is an opportunity for me to try a new challenge. My one over-riding concern was that I wanted to make sure that I wasn't leaving my beloved club in the lurch. I had no need to be concerned as it transpired because Jason Kerr had been working alongside me in the second eleven; he was working as my number two. He was also providing medical support to the players[1] as well, as he had the relevant qualification…and obviously, he has a cricket background. Somerset Cricket Club has quite a small staff complement and as a result, many members of the staff carry out a number of roles. I was comfortable that if I was to go, the position I was vacating was secure because Jason could step up quite easily and he was safe in the knowledge that he could call on the services of his colleagues should the need arise.

I ask Andy how long it took from handing in his notice to leaving the UK. "…. I found out that Suzie was pregnant with Jacob. So that threw a bit of a spanner in the works but we were still comfortable with the decision we were making to go out to the UAE; with the caveat that she now wouldn't come out until after Jacob was born, so that he was born in surroundings we were comfortable with and knew, Musgrove hospital….".

"I flew out to the UAE on my own and as part of the joining process undertook medical examinations, completing work visa criteria, living in a hotel for four weeks, whilst going through the joining process also looking for appropriate accommodation, which was a challenge, to settle into".

How long were you there before she gave birth and came out? "I think I went out to the UAE in May and Jacob was born a month premature in August. It was quite a difficult birth, and he had to spend two weeks in the Intensive Care Unit (ICU). I recall clearly, I had been out during the night and the phone rang about 2 am local time; it was Suzy's mum. "Suzy's gone into labour; can you get back?"

"Without hesitation, thinking it would be easy, I replied; Sure, I will get back today. Little did I know how much red tape would be involved, in order to get an exit visa from the UAE Military; the papers I had to have signed by different levels of authority, just to get out of the country? I spent the next four hours, driving around various Military establishments, waking up high-ranking UAE officers, obtaining their signatures on documents, which would enable me to fly home.

Determined to get back, with the thought of being there for Jacob's birth driving me on, I managed, with great difficulty to obtain every signature I needed.

Finally, and with great haste, I drove to Dubai International airport and bought myself a British Airways return ticket.

My mind was racing; what if he was born before I got there? Would I miss the birth? Would he hold on until I got there?

Eight long hours later, we landed at Heathrow and I hired a car to drive to Taunton, all the way thinking, hold on Jacob.

After what seemed an age, I arrived at Musgrove hospital. I parked the car and ran up to the maternity ward, rushed through the doors and found my way to the labour room, where I found Suzy sucking on the gas and air, her mum holding her hand. With a sigh of relief, I exclaimed, I've made it.

Suzy's Mum was by her bedside, I hugged and thanked her and told her I would stay with Suzy now; my shift was just starting…

As it turned out there was no rush to get back from Dubai! After several hours, Jacob was born; he was tiny and looked so fragile! For someone so small, he let out a loud cry! The midwife took hold of him and gave him to Suzy, who hugged him to her breast for a few moments. The midwife then allowed me to cut the cord before she took Jacob away to the incubator. The next time I saw him, he was in the ICU, tubes everywhere.

It transpired, with Jacob being so premature, his lungs hadn't developed properly, He remained in the hospital for 10 days, before Suzy brought him home.

We returned to the subject of Andy and his profound love of cricket and the difficult position, in which he found himself. I asked him; "So had you made a conscious choice then, that you were quite prepared to leave cricket behind you? I only ask because that was a quite momentous decision".

He responded; ".... well if you think about how tempting the opportunity was for me out in Dubai and the fact that if I could stay there for 10 years, Suzy and I could consider retiring"

Eventually, Suzy and her mother flew out to Dubai to join Andy, her mother accompanying Suzy to help her look after Jacob and support her in managing the transition to life in Dubai. After about ten days or so, Suzy's mother flew back to England.

With Jacob being so very young and many of the other women, mothers to older children amongst the ex-pat community, Suzy found it very difficult to adapt to a very different culture. Unsurprisingly, nurturing a small child is challenging at the best of times and as much as Andy helped, as and when he could, without an independent means of transport, Suzy found it difficult to mix with the other ex-pat women and children. Andy recalls that the traffic was frenetic and this, allied with the intense daytime heat and humidity would have proven more stressful for Suzy. The new life was proving a huge challenge and they needed to consider other options.

During the time that Andy and Suzy were planning what their life would be like in Dubai, they had already agreed that they would return to Taunton, to celebrate Christmas with friends and family. However, when they were planning the move back to Dubai, Suzy told Andy that she would not accompany him, preferring instead to raise Jacob at home.

I asked Andy if this decision had any effect on their marriage but he was adamant, saying; "No we were strong and I was determined to find a new option for us to build our lives around".

Andy returned to Dubai alone, still thinking that if he could stay out there for a good length of time, then he would be in a position to consider retiring.

---o0o---

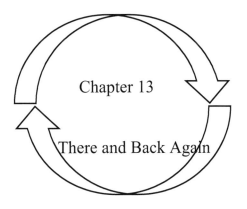

Chapter 13

There and Back Again

Chapter 13

There and Back Again

In the year, that Andy worked in the UAE he assiduously maintained his interest in the world of cricket, both by maintaining contact with his friends at Somerset and through the wider world of the cricket community.

He recalls; "I'd always maintained contact with club captain Ian Blackwell and I talked on the phone, emailed and texted with the Head Coach Garaway, because you know, whether you like it or not this club is deep-rooted in you and even though I was on the other side of the world…it was and is in my blood. I suppose you could say that I had an 'invested interest' in what was going on back here but that wasn't the only reason why I wanted to maintain regular contact. I had a real affinity…a bond with Somerset. He recalls; "…I'm in constant communication with senior players, junior players, Garras (Mark Garaway) and keeping up with how things are going at the club. Therefore, I was up to speed with a number of things that were going on".

Through these regular conversations, Andy became aware that the ECB was on the lookout for a Senior Analyst; one who would function also as an assistant coach to Duncan Fletcher. The vacancy had arisen because the previous incumbent, Tim Boon had resigned after a restructure within the England setup following the successful Ashes defeat of the old rival, Australia by two tests to one. Leicestershire had offered Boon the coach's position as successor to James Whitaker.

Andy had watched the Ashes from Dubai and "…was hooked…" He remembers the excitement and anticipation of each test match and of beating the 'oldest test adversary'.

Freddie Flintoff comforting Aussie fast Bowler Brett Lee, following England's Ashes victory
©The Guardian

He was also hooked on how well Somerset were doing in the T20.

Andy decided, also, to apply for the post of Senior Analyst but his good friend Mark Garaway 'was offered the position'. As disappointed as Andy was, he knew that Mark's appointment to the ECB had created a vacancy at Somerset, the club that he loved. During one of their regular conversations, he asked Mark if he would put in a good word for him at Somerset.

Whilst out in the UAE Andy had been actively "...exploring opportunities..." back in England and through the conversations he'd had with Rosey and a couple of the other key stakeholders at the club, he had the opportunity to come back to Somerset as Head Coach.

Rosey had already decided that his first choice for the position of Head Coach, should he become available, was Andy. He recognised that his proven analytical and diligent approach to everything he accomplished, his knowledge of the game and the mutual respect between Andy and the playing staff was ideal and dovetailed perfectly with the strategic direction, that the club wanted to pursue. Moreover, although it was a wonderful opportunity for Andy, Rosey considered it was an ideal opportunity for the club too. Andy recalls it slightly differently;

---oOo---

Head Coach

Andy looks pensive as he recalls his first few days as Head Coach; "…the reality suddenly hit me…. what if?"

He continues; "So, what do I do if it doesn't work? What am I going to do next? I had just given up a two-year contract, with quite significant earning opportunities in the UAE"; then that familiar look comes into Andy's eyes as he recalls; "No, I will make it work; find a way to make it work. I got over that quite quickly and just threw myself into the role. I love throwing myself into my work". I interject; "Was Ian Blackwell (Blackie) still your captain"? "Yes, but he was injured at the time; *author's note*: *(Blackie, currently an umpire on the ECB list, said at the time; "I had it all last year (2005) really. I had an operation in 2006 and it never healed properly after that. It just got worse and worse last year. It was fine for batting and bowling, but every time I threw it was like a dagger in the arm.").*

Andy continues; "So, he was club captain, but he actually wasn't available for selection, so we asked Matthew Wood to step up.

We had a pre-season tour to South Africa arranged and I had considered that it was a good opportunity to get everyone together into one location and get to know them better…and see how they all functioned together in a confined space. It was a worthwhile exercise, revolution not evolution, if you like because it accelerated the opportunity, we had to understand how we're going to work together in the coming season".

In 2005, the team had won the Twenty20 Cup but sadly finished one off the bottom of the Second Division Championship.

"The Somerset Sabres had finished mid-table in the Totesport Sunday League, Division 2 as well, so we had really struggled. What a welcome for the new Head Coach!"

I interrupt Andy; "the thing is though, you're the Head Coach; the guys that go out on the pitch are the ones with the bat and the ball". He replies, "…but the results of the team reflect on the Head Coach - the Manager and that's part of the responsibility and that's okay as I'm happy with that". I ask Andy a loaded question; "So why didn't they

let you go then after you finished bottom?"

"Because I think again, through effective communication and collaboration with key players and an effective working relationship with Rosey, we could see what we had, what we needed, to progress and how we were we going to get where we needed to be as a club. Another very good decision was the appointment of Richard Gould as CEO".

Head Coach

"Through the winter months, we assembled a small management team together and began to map out how we were going to get to a point where we could make this club a real sporting 'tour de force' again. We discussed many options and one that emerged was to use the services of an external consultant, who could come into the club with a fresh pair of eyes and new ideas; so, Richard Gould contacted Alan Sears from Vybrant, a consultancy based in Berkshire".

I met with Alan at a quaint Bistro Pub called The Withies, in Compton and over a pleasant lunch, we discussed his company's involvement with Andy and Somerset.

Alan takes up the story; "I had a phone call, out of the blue, from Richard Gould who said, hello, I understand you do leadership development. I asked if this was executive coaching for him; he said, no, it's the playing squad here at Somerset County Cricket. I said I'll get in the car and come straight down to meet you (*Author's note: It was obvious from our discussion that Alan was really very keen to do this*). I haven't ever been particularly interested in cricket as such you know, I'll watch a test match if England are playing and that's usually about it. However, I am fascinated by the number of times people bring the lessons learned from sport into business. I have to be honest if I say that it doesn't always work because the motivations are often very different. It 'goes without saying' that the ordinary person at work is not motivated in the same way as a professional sportsperson is but I was very keen to see if I could take lessons from business into professional sport."

"So, I went down to Taunton, met Richard and Andy Hurry and spent a full day at the club and I got on extremely well with Andy Hurry and he and Richard agreed that I should meet and talk to as many of the squad as possible in the day. Andy Hurry and I got on well

Andy had lined up James Hildreth, Pete Trego and a number of others and - at the last minute, Andy Hurry said he had persuaded Andy Caddick to speak to me, but that Caddick had only a few minutes.

The discussions with Trego and Hildreth and the other members of the squad who were good enough to talk to me were positive and many issues and bullet points for further discussion were agreed.

Later in the day, Andy Caddick and I met in Andy Hurry's office. The meeting started with a glare from Andy and him asking me; "What's all this about then"? I explained why the club had engaged me and I started by saying I appreciate you are pushed for time so perhaps I can start by asking you to tell me how morale is at the club.

He looked me in the eye and said; "**it's shit**"! I took my pen and I wrote down the letters about four inches high.

I wrote **ⅬⅠHS S、ⅬⅠ 'ⅠO** so that he can see upside down, that I'd just written exactly what he'd said, which I think might just have slightly surprised him. I think he may have started with the opinion, not unlike yours, about consultants in general. (*Author's note; my experience of consultants is that one pays for them to look at your watch and tell you the time*)

I don't know quite what it was that kept the conversation going but after about half an hour, somebody stuck their head around the door and said, your car is here. In the end, we'd talked for about 45 minutes, with Andy resisting about three or four calls telling him he needed to go. We achieved a rapport of sorts but the thing I remember him saying, specifically, in that first interview is, '…the thing you've got to understand is there is no team in cricket, it's an entirely individual game. We're all based on our averages…'

But here's the most rewarding part; pre-season 2008, at the last workshop I did with them, Andy Caddick stood up in the room, turned to the rest of the squad and said; "I just want you all to know, this is the best fucking team I've ever played in or met or anything else" and I thought Hallelujah!

As it transpired, Andy Caddick became a real leader during these workshops and one of the main things, which we; that is the squad and me, established in the sessions, was the concept of 'no blame'. I also think one of the most interesting conversations they had as a squad, was when somebody, I can't remember who it was, put their hand up and said;" …there's too much what we called banter in the dressing room but it's not banters. We criticise each other and tear each other down…." Alan continues; "This comment led to quite a vociferous discussion on the value of dressing room banter, but in the end those in favour of it agreed to moderate it and make sure others did not feel criticised – which was a big factor in maintaining morale."

There was already the nucleus of a tight squad, I consider myself as just the enabler and the sessions we had been involved in, allowed the honesty and the squad's character to come to the forefront.

Team ethos is a living, breathing entity, albeit intangible and it is essentially self-fulfilling. I can only say that I am delighted to have played a small part in Somerset's ongoing success. It was a real revelation for me too, as I have been able to take some of the findings and conclusions from the squad sessions and use them to drive change in the boardrooms of commercial businesses.

Alan Sears

Andy fully supported Alan's appointment, recalling that; "...I was determined to get the club back on an upward trend. It wasn't a one-man effort by the way. It was very much Brian and Richard Gould's involvement, which helped achieve the improvement; once again

Andy is not seeking any recognition for the improvement in Somerset's fortunes.

We facilitated a number of meetings and through this process and with Alan's help, we were clearer on what our identity was, how we wanted to go about 'our business' and what type of players we wanted. How did we measure success? What is achievable and how long before we see improvement? It was very inclusive. Alan worked methodically, through a very sturdy pragmatic process, which enabled us to understand the way forward. It is satisfying to know that Alan has been able to use some of the knowledge gained at the club in his commercial work.

I ask; "What positives and what learnings did you take from this consultancy exercise"? Andy responded; "How do you win a game of cricket? Well, you become more skilful, developing better skills than the opposition. Okay, so how are we going to develop our skills? There was a lot of emphasis on how & what we coached; how we supported our players, both mentally and drove their physical development. And actually, when everyone else was taking four months off through the winter, we're going to be in training for those four months and working hard in the gym, developing our players and growing a mind-set to being the best we can be".

"And the key secret, which was facilitated by Alan, was making sure Brian Rose and Richard Gould were fully involved, in there with all the key stakeholders. These included some of the senior players and up and coming

James Hildreth

players, Caddy, James Hildreth (Hildy) and Peter Trego (Tregs) for example; not everybody of course but making sure all the key stakeholders were influencing how we're going to operate". "Was there any resistance to this regime"? I ask. "No, not a bit; just remember where we were starting from, we were down, we were low. People don't want to be associated with failure; they want to be associated with success - if one wins then we all win.

Here's an example, if one of the players, not involved in the strategy meetings was to say, "…why are we having to come into the gym every day…" Hildy, Tregs, or AN Other can say…because we're doing this…or…because this is how this will benefit the team…. "There was complete buy-in by all of the players and they supported each other. It doesn't have to come from the Head Coach all the time. Obviously, to cement that, you have to get some success early on and we did really well, nailed the first two games but if we had lost those opening games, it might have been a different story, a different outcome.

However, we just kept winning and eventually won the Second Division title with a new record tally of 266 points, 52 points clear of second place. We lost one match all season and finished with the highest number of batting points in both divisions. The winning mentality was beginning to ingrain itself into the team.

Andy unassumingly tells me; "what cannot be over-emphasised though is the 'JL effect'. Justin Langer is a superlative leader and there is no doubt that he was a catalyst in the improvement in the team's performance". Rosey signed JL for Somerset in July 2006, initially for six weeks. However, before returning to Australia, he agreed to return to the Club as Captain for the 2007 season. In the end, he remained with the club for three years, assuming the captaincy from 2007. Under his captaincy, Marcus Trescothick and Andrew Caddick featured in the leading averages for batting and bowling respectively.

On 1 January 2007, he announced that he would retire from Test cricket after the fifth Ashes Test against England, starting at the Sydney Cricket Ground the following day. He wanted to continue to play first-class

cricket in England and the announcements were synchronised to the world that he had agreed to return to Somerset in 2007 as captain. He had said during his retirement announcement that he was relishing the return to Somerset; saying, "There's an amazing challenge at Somerset, I've got great regard for Andy Hurry, the Head Coach over there, and I'm really looking forward to the challenge.

2007 marked Andy's second season as Head Coach and the first season for JL as his Captain. Justin, who by this time knew the team well, had played the whole of the 2006 season under the captaincy of Cameron White and his first match for Somerset took place against Devon at Exmouth on 21st June.

Head Coach

Coaching team 2006: Andy Hurry Jason Kerr
Pete Sanderson Daz Veness Brian Rose

---o0o---

2007 Season Div. 2 Results

Date	Match	Venue	Result
18th April	Somerset v Middlesex	County Ground,	D
25th April	Leicestershire v Somerset	Grace Road	W
2nd May	Somerset v Derbyshire	County Ground	D
8th May	Northants v Somerset	County Ground	D
23rd May	Somerset v Gloucestershire	County Ground	W
30th May	Middlesex v Somerset	Lord's	L
6th June	Somerset v Leicestershire	County Ground	W*
15th June	Gloucestershire v Somerset	County Ground	W*
13th July	Somerset v Northants	County Ground	W
20th July	Somerset v Essex	County Ground	D
25th July	Derbyshire v Somerset	County Ground	W
8th August	Notts v Somerset	Trent Bridge	W
14th August	Glamorgan v Somerset	Sophia Gardens	D
30th August	Somerset v Glamorgan	County Ground	W
5th Sept	Essex v Somerset Secured the Division 2 Title	Ford County Ground	W
19th Sept	Somerset v Notts	County Ground	W*

Courtesy of Cricket Archive

The 2007 season saw Somerset win 10 of their 16 fixtures, three of which they achieved with an innings to spare (marked thus *). They lost just one match, away from home at Lord's to Middlesex and drew five.

Head Coach: The Third Year

In 2007, Langer returned to the team as club Captain. Somerset's season began brightly, including a county-record 850/7 declared against Middlesex in their first Championship match, but a few weeks later Somerset were on the wrong end of a huge total when they conceded 801/8 declared to Derbyshire.

However, they recovered well from this setback and achieved promotion, returning to Division 1 of the Championship for the first time since 2002, after beating Essex at Chelmsford with five sessions to spare.

It is Andy's modest and unassuming nature, which will not allow him to take full credit for this incredible turnaround in Somerset's fortunes. It is also self-evident that the meticulous training regime and schedule, the shrewd team selections, the camaraderie, the dedication of the players to the club and the mutual respect all of the players had, played a major part in their success. The work done with Alan Sears had reaped benefits and Somerset were once again one of the best teams in the country

---oOo---

Head Coach

County Championship: Division Two 2007

	Team	Played	W	Tie	L	D	A	Bat	Bowl	Points
1	Somerset	16	10	0	1	5	0	65	41	266
2	Notts	16	6	0	3	7	0	60	43	214½
3	Middx	16	6	0	2	8	0	35	43	192½
4	Essex	16	6	0	4	6	0	40	36	182
5	Northants	16	5	0	5	6	0	44	38	176
6	Derby	16	3	0	5	8	0	30	44	147
7	Glos	16	3	0	5	8	0	32	37	139½
8	Leics	16	2	0	8	5	1	32	35	115
9	Glam	16	1	0	9	5	1	26	37	92½

Table Courtesy of CricketArchive

County Championship: Division One 2008

Team	Pld	W	L	T	D	A	Bat	Bowl	Adj	
Durham	16	6	3	0	6	1	37	41	0	190
Notts	16	5	3	0	7	1	37	43	0	182
Hants	16	5	4	0	7	0	33	47	0	178
Somerset	16	3	2	0	11	0	44	44	0	174
Lancs	16	5	2	0	8	1	24	40	0	170
Sussex	16	2	2	0	12	0	45	38	0	159
Yorks	16	2	5	0	9	0	50	45	0	159
Kent	16	4	6	0	6	0	30	44	0	154
Surrey	16	0	5	0	10	1	45	36	1	124

Table Courtesy of CricketArchive

The Met Office© records that, *'March and April 2008 both had above average rainfall over the UK, with March having 128% of average rainfall and April having 109% of average rainfall'*.

The 2008 season was a bit of a 'washout' for the game of cricket all together. Of the one hundred and forty-four games played, seventy-six games ended in a draw, with the South of the country experiencing the wettest weather. Sussex,

Surrey and Somerset had thirty-three draws between them. Somerset finished the season in fourth place, just sixteen points behind the champions, Durham.

---o0o---

2009

If 2008 was disappointing in terms of the weather, 2009 was disastrous with only twenty-nine of the one hundred and forty-four matches ending in a positive result. Eighty-six matches ended in draws, with the inclement weather spread equally over the country. However, Somerset finished in third place, with twelve draws from their sixteen matches. Although the same could be said for other teams equally affected, it could still be postulated that the poor playing conditions *potentially* denied the club precious points and a crack at the title, which was retained by Durham. At the end of the season Andy signed a new contract, which tied him to Somerset as head coach until 2012.

County Championship: Division One 2009
Table courtesy of Cricket Archive

Team	Pld	W	L	D	T	A	Bat	Bwl	Adj	Pts
Durham (C)	16	8	0	8	0	0	49	48	−1	240
Notts	16	4	2	10	0	0	56	41	0	193
Somerset	16	3	1	12	0	0	50	43	−1	182
Lancs	16	4	2	10	0	0	35	44	0	175
Warks	16	3	3	10	0	0	54	38	0	174
Hampshire	16	3	3	10	0	0	50	40	−3	169
Yorkshire	16	2	2	12	0	0	46	44	0	166
Sussex (R)	16	2	6	8	0	0	45	39	−1	143
Worcs (R)	16	0	10	6	0	0	30	40	0	94

Notable milestones from 2009 were:

- Hildy passed 4000 runs in first-class matches

- Tregs reached 100 wickets in County Championship matches

---oOo---

© ECB

2010 and England: The First Time

The 2010 season saw Somerset County Cricket Club competing in three domestic competitions; the first division of the County Championship, the Clydesdale Bank 40 and the Friends Provident t20. They finished as runners up in the County Championship by, it must be said, the slimmest of margins. They finished second in the Friends Provident t20 and they reached the final of the Clydesdale Bank 40 competition.

County Championship: Division One 2010

Team	P	W	L	D	T	A	BAT	Bowl	Adj	Pts
Notts	16	7	5	4	0	0	47	43	0	214
Somerset	16	6	2	8	0	0	53	41	0	214
Yorks	16	6	2	8	0	0	41	42	0	203
Lancs	16	5	3	8	0	0	35	43	0	182
Durham	16	5	3	8	0	0	30	39	0	173
Warks	16	6	9	1	0	0	20	47	0	166
Hants	16	3	6	7	0	0	47	41	0	157
Kent	16	3	7	6	0	0	42	44	-1	151
Essex	16	2	6	8	0	0	29	43	-2	126

Table Courtesy of CricketArchive

During the time that Andy had been completing his Level 4 coaching certificate, he had forged a close relationship with his mentor, Gordon Lord and during the many conversations between the two men, Andy had expressed his desire to coach at England level. Andy takes up the story; "I'd always expressed an interest with level four coaching manager Gordon Lord, my desire to coach at International level. My aspirations were to coach England. However, Gordon was unsure whether I had the capabilities to coach England and I said no that's what I want to do and I'll find a way. He said to me, you've never even played international cricket and I go, I know but I have other skills that I can bring and if I surround myself with the right people, that won't be an issue. I think he really valued my determination and drive and ambition and I'd also sort of mapped out in my head how, if I did get myself in a position as head coach of England, how I would go about surrounding myself with the right people. I had to have people around me who played the international game because players will want to go and get those experiences from those guys. My role would be to manage the whole program and the team. I kept harping onto him, I need experience, need opportunity and I need to go and find out."

---oOo---

2010 and England: The First Time

England: The First Time

"So, eventually, he organized with Andy Flower, the opportunity for me to go out to the UAE as a CPD (Continuing Professional Development) opportunity. To go out there and observe and just be around the environment but luckily for me, the fielding coach at the time (Richard Halsall); his wife was pregnant, which meant he went home for the birth. And rather than just being in there and just observing I was actually given a key role, which was to oversee the fielding in the one-day series and the T20 series. I wasn't expecting that when I originally got the opportunity. That evolved and then obviously when I got out there, I met with Andy Flower. He gave me a clear remit and again, there was an anxiety, can I really do this? You know, have I got the skills but you don't know. And this is the same for young players. When you pick them, they play first team cricket, of course they want to do it. They don't know if they're good enough until they score a hundred or they take their first wicket, then it's right, yeah okay I belong at this level and very quickly after a short period of time working under

Flower in the England environment. I thought, I can do this. I'm alright, I can do this. And what reinforced that to me was that actually I was talking to Kevin Pietersen, Jimmy Anderson, Stuart Broad and Alastair Cook and they were listening. They were responding to direction that I was giving them. I really respect the fact they gave me that opportunity and it just grew and grew and grew. My confidence grew and again, as I've alluded to it, so that was all fine during the training but leading into the first game I got really nervous".

Andy Flower speaks highly of Andy Hurry; "I'd heard some positive things about Andy from talking to various people in the game and Gordon Lord, Head of Elite Coaching at the ECB, suggested Andy Hurry to me. I trusted Gordon's judgment so I invited Andy out and he was dead keen to come; as soon as he arrived in our group, he made a positive difference".

The coaches that were in the UAE for the tests and the one-day games were –

- **Phil Neale**   Tour Operations Manager

- **Andy Flower**   Head coach (Tests)

- **Richard Halsall**   Fielding coach (Tests)

- **Andy**   Fielding coach (T20 & ODIs)

- **Graham Gooch**   Batting coach

- **David Saker**   Fast bowling coach

- **Mushtaq Ahmed**   Spin bowling coach

- **Bruce French**   Wicket-keeping coach

- **Huw Bevan** Strength & conditioning coach

Andy considered this a once in a lifetime opportunity to work with the senior England team and Andy Flower was delighted with the decision to bring him out because he made a positive impression on everybody he interacted with. I'll let Andy tell it in his own words; "I was of course a little apprehensive with a once in a lifetime opportunity to work with the senior England team ahead of me.

It started well with a delivery of all the Adidas training kit; I was like a boy at Christmas opening the packages and trying all the clothing on, a suitcase, England suit with the three lions embroidered on and a return Business class flight to Abu Dhabi. I was in heaven......

2010 and England: The First Time

I landed in UAE and was picked up and taken to the team hotel, where the England Lions squad and coaching team were all located in preparation of a warm up game against the senior side in preparation for the One day & T20 series vs Pakistan.

It was great to see some familiar faces, especially Kevin Shine who was overseeing the Lions pace bowlers. I was made to feel really welcome.

I received the detail that I would be taken to the Sheikh Zayed stadium to meet up with Andy and the senior squad who were travelling there from Dubai after the Test series to do some physical training and I was to meet up with Andy to be briefed on my role.

I waited at the stadium with anticipation, Andy strolled out to the outfield where I strode towards him and shook his hand with a firm grip, I always believed it was important to have a firm hand shake.

Andy welcomed me and briefed me that I would be responsible for the squads fielding, and asked was I comfortable with that. I'm sure he was nervous in entrusting a complete stranger with this responsibility, however I looked him straight in the eyes and told him,

"I'm all over it, just brief me on what themes you want delivered and I will deliver for you"

I was caught between, excitement and nerves of the thought of being accountable for my role, but I believed I could exceed his expectations. I was introduced to the squad and I could see one or two of the players were thinking; "Who is this?"

I had nothing to do during this first session other than observe the players working, all the time my mind was thinking; "OK, how am I going to see this through successfully?"

"The next day and for a series of days we had scheduled practice sessions and Andy briefed me on when my time would be to work with the players and how long we had for each session.

I chatted to the coaches and narrowed down how I was going to deliver my sessions.

I developed strong relationships with Andy, Hugh Bevan (Strength & Conditioning) & David Saker (Bowling coach) over the first few days and their insights were very useful.

2010 and England: The First Time

Together we hatched a plan to deliver specific sessions around the team's needs, some of which integrated Strength & Conditioning and to be fair to all the players they really gave it everything.

I loved it and we finished all our practices and were ready for the first game.

I have two very strong memories of that series *Firstly*, my nerves on the day of the first ODI.

I went through the normal process of an early breakfast, usually with Sir Alistair Cook, just him and I chatting rubbish over fresh fruit and eggs, obviously not at the same time. I would go to the gym and then back to my room ready to meet the coaches mini bus. The coaches mini bus left for the game earlier than the player's team bus. I was walking back from my room from the gym for a shower and then to get changed, when the nerves hit me!

"What if I broke a player's finger in warm up, what if I couldn't hit the appropriate catches, what if .... what if."

2010 and England: The First Time

I held onto the anxiety on the mini bus and into the ground
"What if…...?"

"It wasn't till I got changed, dragged my fielding bag out
to the outfield, did the nerves, anxiety leave me. "Yes, this
is where I belong, this is what I want to do"

Preparation went well. I sat and watched the game noting
all my observations and really enjoying the win. The boys
and coaches sang the team song, I just watched with pride.
We won a lot during the series and it wasn't long before I
was joining in with the team song too.

Secondly during the last game, Andy came up to me as
soon as the game started and said; "After the game tonight
I want you to review the game with the players". "Sure" I
replied. **** what the **** am I going to say?"

I'd never watched a game so intently; I wrote more down
of what I had observed than I had ever written down. I also
crossed out more. As the game unfolded and we moved
towards winning another game, I must have changed what
I was going to say 30 times.

The game finished, I could feel the anxiety growing, what
a moment in my life was waiting for me just behind the

changing room door. We won, again and it was my moment…

I was very clear what I was going to say, which was about 5% of what I wanted to say. What was said will mostly remain there, but a key message was how honoured I had felt to be given this opportunity and to share being inside the changing room with a winning England Team.

This was honestly, one of the best experiences of my life, it's right up there and I feel honoured to have had the opportunity to have been given the chance to stretch myself at the highest level and to have had the opportunity to get to know the players and staff of that successful series so well.

I returned home with the team after an amazing night of celebration.

Life is about memories and this experience is one I will never forget.

---o0o---

Head Coach: 2011
2011

Andy was now back in the driving seat at Somerset following his brief but successful tour as fielding coach with the England senior team in the United Arab Emirates.

James Hildreth steering a ball behind square on his way to a score of 20 in the 2011 Twenty20 Cup Final against Leicestershire at Edgbaston

Domestically, Somerset finished 4th in the first division of the County Championship in the 2011 season. In all, they competed in three domestic competitions; where they reached the final of the Clydesdale Bank 40 and their third consecutive Friends Life t20 final. However, in global competitions they failed to make it past the group stages in the Caribbean Twenty20 but impressed in the Champions League Twenty20, reaching the semi-finals.

County Championship: Division One 2011

Head Coach: 2011

Team	Pld	W	L	D	T	A	Bat	Bwl	Adj	Pts
Lancs (C)	16	10	4	2	0	0	37	44	-1	246
Warks	16	9	4	3	0	0	46	45	-9	235
Durham	16	8	4	4	0	0	47	45	0	232
Somerset	16	6	7	3	0	0	45	39	0	189
Sussex	16	6	6	4	0	0	34	40	0	182
Notts	16	5	6	5	0	0	35	43	0	173
Worcs	16	4	11	1	0	0	31	44	0	142
Yorks (R)	16	3	6	7	0	0	34	37	-2	138
Hants (R)	16	3	6	7	0	0	30	36	-8	127

Table Courtesy of CricketArchive

---oOo---

Head Coach: 2012

An indication of the continuing improvements in Somerset's performances under Andy as Head Coach could not be more evident than in 2012. Despite the club suffering from injuries to several players, resulting in many enforced squad changes, Somerset missed the championship spot by just 24 runs.

County Championship: Division One 2012

Team	Pld	W	L	D	T	A	Bat	Bwl	Adj	Pts
Warks (C)	16	6	1	9	0	0	43	45	0	211
Somerset	16	5	1	10	0	0	32	45	0	187
Middlesex	16	5	4	7	0	0	33	38	0	172
Sussex	16	5	5	6	0	0	28	41	0	167
Notts	16	4	2	10	0	0	26	43	0	163
Durham	16	5	5	5	0	1	18	45	-4	157
Surrey	16	3	4	8	0	1	26	40	-2	139
Lancs (R)	16	1	5	10	0	0	25	35	0	106
Worcs (R)	16	1	8	7	0	0	17	42	0	96

Table Courtesy of CricketArchive

---o0o---

England

© ECB

The Second Time

England: The Second Time

Andy recalls his first days as Head Coach; "I was naive in 2006 but I still backed myself, that I could deliver. I still remember that day, when I walked into that changing room on the first morning, I wasn't really sure how it was all going to pan out and was I really good enough?

I didn't know. And that's the reality of it. I didn't know but I was going to find out pretty quickly. I had some anxieties but I knew the things I could control. let's make sure we're organized and let's make sure we get some structure around the practice sessions. Let's make sure we're clear around how we're gonna look to play our cricket. Sadly, as the 2006 season unfolded, it went from bad to worse.

And at the end of that season, we had to sit down and review what was holding us back, which we went through in a lot of detail. And Alan Sears helped me massively understand the importance of team dynamics. So that was an area that grew straight away, the value of how the team operated and what was it all going to unite around that was really important. So, it was a massive lesson very early on. Identifying the need around good young players that were-coming through and how you can use and b rely on the senior guys to help them. 2007 is evidence that this strategy worked, inasmuch that they helped massively to accelerate the young players' development.

Having got that success of winning the Second Division County Championship with a very, very strong side, I felt my man management skills really evolved. My understanding of some of the demands on the players and the challenges of the season grew massively. Therefore, I was growing a lot of awareness developing through experiences some skills to be able to predict some of those things were going to be happening. Subsequently we could put some plans in place. So again, we did really well the following year.

However, after 7 years as Head Coach, life was about to change for Andy once again.

At the end of the 2012 season, Brian Rose stood down as DOC and in December of that year, the Somerset committee appointed South African Dave Nosworthy as the new DOC.

England: The Second Time

Nosworthy immediately set about introducing significant changes to the coaching and management structure at the club. The most radical change - and the one, which was to have the most significance for Andy - was the loss of the role of Head Coach as Nosworthy had subsumed this responsibility into role of DOC and decided to split the role into two; an 'assistant' batting coach and a bowling coach.

David Houghton, formerly of Derbyshire, was brought in as assistant batting coach, 'assisting' Nosworthy and former academy coach Jason Kerr took on the role of bowling coach.

Referring to Jason Kerr and Houghton, Andy is quoted at the time as saying; "It's two great signings for the club; it's so positive to have two quality and experienced coaches coming in to support Dave at the top. They're great attributes for the players to have. It's something the players have been crying out for a number of years."

Andy also said that the change to his role was always planned; "I did expect it to happen. I have ambitions at this club to go further; I have been working with the first team, [*in various roles*] since 2001, so it's a bit of a shock to the system not being involved with them any more.....however, I see this move as an opportunity for me, selfishly, to develop areas and experiences that can help me go even further in the management structure of the club. Jason has been an excellent coach and it's great seeing them (*the academy players*) come through. Their motivation and enthusiasm to become first-class cricketers really excites me."

I asked Andy, whether with the benefit of hindsight, he viewed this period in his life any differently.

[Author's note] In the time that I have got to know Andy, I have become more and more impressed by his clarity of thought and thorough understanding of human nature. As he began re-telling the series of events surrounding the appointment of Dave Nosworthy, these traits shone through like a beacon.

He began; "I don't think Dave was a good fit for this club. That's just my opinion and that's not his fault. He applied for a job, he applied for a position based on his record and he was given the opportunity. And I learned a lot of very useful things from Dave. My experience with him has helped me grow as a coach. But I think what's important for any employer is to make sure when they're employing external candidates, that they get the right fit for that environment. This environment has been going on since 1875 and it has its own way of operating; people in it are unique and it's important that you get the right fit for that. (*Author's note: Founded in 1875, Somerset was initially regarded as a minor county until official first-class status was gained in 1895*).

Because if you look at how Trevor Bayliss has gone into the England one day team, he was the perfect fit for that group of players. They could have got another coach in and even though they are the same group of players, there could have been a totally different outcome if it wasn't a right fit. And in my view, Dave Nosworthy's got a huge number of strengths. He just wasn't the right fit for this club at that time and I think it's important the lesson I took away from that is that you can have a great CV, you could be a great person, but it's about what that group of people need at that time to get them to where you want them to get to. And it was a journey that was useful for everyone to go through. Dave, the coaches, the players, because if nothing else, it just reinforced that they needed to operate differently.

So that was good learning for everybody. It wasn't a mistake in any way. It just didn't work out. It just wasn't the right fit. I ask him; "So what did you think about his strategy of splitting the head coach's role"? "Well, obviously I was the head coach at the time". "And you said some nice things at the time". "Yeah, and that's fine. because I've learned a lot off Dave Nosworthy and that's his and the committee's decision that they, go with split roles. There was a Head Coach and Director of Cricket role and then he amalgamated the DOC and Head Coaches roles. When he did that, did he speak to, you? No, he told me that he's going to the committee to tell them that the club needs to operate in a different way.

He needed more responsibility to influence the team more. So, he didn't think that you'd done a good job? Yeah, basically I got fired from being head coach, but the interesting thing is, that the club did the same thing again when they appointed Matt Maynard, doing the same thing, a dual role. But the learning, which they did take; credit to the club, is actually that doesn't work. You need to have a split role. It needs to have a head coach that's able to concentrate on the cricket and managing the players because that's demanding. You have to have 100% energy to that and you need a separate role for someone to oversee the strategic aspects of the club".

"So, what have you learned and in particular, taken from this specific episode in your life"?

"Well, the learning was – well, I was very disappointed because I still felt we had a distance to travel and I felt my time had been cut short. I respect the fact that people 'make a decision' based on what they believe is in the best interest of the club. So that's okay but disappointing. Interestingly the learning I took from that is you never ever burn any of your bridges ever, because you never know what the future looks like. And if I'd been challenging or difficult, the opportunity for me to come back [here] would have been closed. And I always wanted to be here. I always wanted to be at some stage, whether it's five years, 10 years, 20 years' time. I want it to be sat in this chair as director cricket help shape the direction of the club.

And you know, the club had also looked after me when they moved me from head coach. They moved me to second 11 Head Coach, Academy Director and the Director of High Performance. This covered a lot of areas that I hadn't got a lot of experience in. I got to understand the role of the Second Team Head Coach and the demands that puts on you. I'd got to work with adolescent players and the academy. Skills I thought I had and actually I was a million miles away from having those skills, I grew those skills to a level that got me the opportunity to go and be head coach for the England Under 19s. Now I've come back to Somerset and I've been the Strength and Conditioning Coach, I've been the Second 11 Head Coach, I've been the Head Coach; I've been the Academy Director and now I'm Director of Cricket I have an awareness of some of the challenges and demands of those roles, but also I know how important it is having been in each of those roles. How important it is for the DOC to have an invested interest in those?

England: The Second Time

Brian Rose demonstrated to me when I was Head Coach how important it is for the Director of Cricket to have a strong relationship with the Head Coach. So now when I'm speaking to Steve Snell as Academy Director, I understand the challenges and demands and how important it is for me to have a relationship with him to make him feel valued. I understand that the demands of Greg Kennis the Second Team Coach is having because I've been in that position - how important it is for me to support him through that. The same with Jason as Head Coach, I understand Joel Tratt, the S & C coach's needs, I was in that situation myself and I'm very, very fortunate to have had all those experiences and even though at the time I was frustrated and disappointed to lose my job as Head Coach, it provided me with new learning, an opportunity to develop new skills and has now enabled me to go on and get an England U19 team job, get some exposure within the England environment, come back here and be able to manage this whole operation more effectively. How lucky am I"?

"And do you know the other interesting thing about the whole experience? I also understand, when I'm talking to players, when I'm not renewing their contracts, how devastating it is for them sat in that chair because I felt that devastation and it gives me an opportunity, through my experiences, to share; ' ...I know how you're feeling...'. It doesn't always land but I can have the conversation and then share some of my journey that got me back to being in this position".

He looks up to his left as if to emphasis this point; "But then I also understand that once they walk through that door, I've got a responsibility to keep following up with them, check in and see how they're doing, trying to help them to get back on their journey. I've got a lot of experience that allows me to deal with some very difficult situations.

So Nosworthy carried out the roles of DOC and Head Coach for two years, until, as Nick Hoult writes in the Telegraph newspaper; '*Matthew Maynard will today be announced as the new head coach at Somerset. The former England and Glamorgan batsman has landed his first head coaching role in county cricket since leaving Glamorgan in 2010 replacing Dave Nosworthy, who left the club after two seasons at the end of the championship campaign. Nosworthy left two years into a three-year contract after Somerset fell away in the county championship and one-day performances failed to improve'.*

Sitting opposite each other, I sip at a cup of coffee. During sips, I ask Andy; "So what happened to your role when Nosworthy left"?

Andy continues; "So the bottom line is, my gut feeling is that the club wanted to make sure I was okay when I lost my position as Head Coach. They created this role as Director of High Performance to give it some Kudos, some value attached to it. And there was a lot of value attached to it. And I grew a lot through the experience and I really enjoyed the role".

Me; "So the club didn't set you up to fail"?

"No, No! And then the opportunity for the Nineteens came up, I went through the interview process and I got the job, erm at the backend of it".

I asked Andy how the job came about.

England: The Second Time

"Gordon Lord rang me and told me about the role; he said that I should seriously consider putting my name forward and applying. Initially, I thought it would involve me spending too much time away from home, travelling regularly to Loughborough. I spoke to Amy who gave me her full support and I asked Jacob if he would be ok with me being away from home so much. He was so excited, "will you be working with Joe Root", "No I said but I'll be working with the next generation of Joe Roots" With their unconditional backing, I decided to apply".

Did you have to give a presentation? "No, it was a theory-based interview",

And where was the interview held? "It was held at Loughbough in an office in Burleigh Court and I was interviewed by Paul Downton (ECB Cricket director) Gordon Lord, Dave Parsons (ECB Performance Director) & Martyn Moxon (Yorkshire DOC)". How long did the interview last? "…oh, about an hour".

And what would you say are your highlights in the 3 years in the role?

Andy recalls; "Well…. I went in there thinking I knew how to get the best out of teenagers but I went into an environment where there were coaches and administrators who had vastly more experience than me in working with adolescent athletes. Previously there had been an under 19 and under 17 program and they'd just disbanded the under 17 programme, so there were a number of coaches and staff who'd lost their jobs but the ECB had still retained them. I was then given the choice to retain some of those staff or release them; I'd decided that I wanted to retain their expertise because I knew I needed to lean on them and learn from them.

Working with adolescents; I thought I knew all there was to know about working with them! What did I know? Iain Brunnschwiler an expert in working with adolescent athletes and the head coach of the England Under-17s taught me so much. The U17s had been disbanded but I wanted Iain to stay in the team. As it turned out, it was a decision that paid off massively.

A lot of the processes and strategies that I introduced and currently use in my present job at Somerset, I learnt from Mo BoBat who went on to Lead on the ECB Talent ID and is now the ECB Performance Director, he was our Operations Manager.

England: The Second Time

There was so much expertise in the members of my team. Tim Boon's experience and input was invaluable. Steve McCaig, the Australian, who was brought in as England physio and who had the infamous confrontation with his hero, Ricky Ponting in the 2009 Ashes, at Cardiff.

I also had the privilege of working with the Sports Science & Medical staff; comprising Rob Ahmun the S&C coach, Mike Mustoe & Hannah Jowitt analysts and Matt Hipwell, our administrator.

Special memories are leading several competitive cricket series in Australia, India, Sri Lanka and the ICC Cricket World Cup U19 in Bangladesh.

Other treasured memories are working with special, talented young cricketers such as Haseeb Hameed, Sam Curran, Mason Crane, Tom Banton, Matt Parkinson and Ollie Pope who have all gone on to play for the senior side. Being head of England's development programme can have enormous benefits, working with the cream of young cricket and even though Andy was totally immersed in the day-to-day running of the programme, it can also be a lonely place.

England: The Second Time

Writing in the Daily Mail in 2016, Richard Gibson wrote;
Andy Hurry dropped [Haseeb] *Hameed from England's U19s squad earlier this year... Andy Hurry, head of England's development programme, informed Hameed of his omission in a Colombo hotel room last December, and instead of sulking, the Lancashire teenager used the snub as a motivating factor. 'It was a very tough conversation to have with someone so passionate about his aspirations...but he took the news very maturely and it says something about him that he used it as a driving force to play Test cricket. 'No matter what obstacles are put in Haseeb's way, he finds a way to overcome them.'*

England: The Second Time

Iain Brunnschwiler   Mo BoBat

Steve McCaig in 'discussion' with Aussie Skipper Ricky Ponting, who questioned his loyalty to Australia

Steve McCaig   Rob Ahmun

Paul Downton   Dave Parsons

Andy with England U19's in 2015

England: The Second Time

©ESPN wrote of Andy at the time; '*His time as Somerset coach brought a period of hugely consistent performance from the team but they had no silverware to show for their efforts. In his new role, Hurry will work with the England Under19 team as well as the county cricket academy and coaches.*

"*I am departing with a very heavy heart having enjoyed the most incredible journey at Somerset since arriving in 2001,*" Hurry said. "*I am very proud of the small part I have played in building this magnificent club and it has been an immense privilege to lead and coach an amazing group of players over many years.*"

"*I am incredibly grateful for the help and support of the club, coaches and members and I wish Somerset the very best for the future. Whilst it is difficult to leave, I am hugely excited by this new appointment and the opportunity to help build the next generation of England players.*"

Paul Downton, the managing director of England cricket, said; "This is a new position which reflects the importance we place on developing talent and our desire to fully integrate the work of County academies with the existing programmes for age-group cricketers in place at the NCPC (National Cricket Performance Centre)."'

---o0o---

References

County Championship: Division One 2019

Pos	Team	Pld	W	L	D	Tie	Bat	Bowl	Pts
1	Essex (C)	14	9	1	4	0	26	38	228
2	Somerset	14	9	3	2	0	25	38	217
3	Hampshire	14	5	3	6	0	31	36	176
4	Kent	14	5	5	4	0	36	36	172
5	Yorkshire	14	5	4	5	0	24	36	165
6	Surrey	14	2	6	6	0	33	38	133
7	Warks	14	3	6	5	0	26	32	131
8	Notts	14	0	10	4	0	16	32	67

Table Courtesy of CricketArchive

Somerset sat atop the Championship table for much of the season and their success and the title remained firmly in their grip, if they managed to maintain their good form.

The penultimate match against Hampshire at the Rose Bowl was a portent of things to come and it seems that any stardust, with which the team had been sprinkled up to that point, had been blown away by an ill wind as Hampshire's tall 32-year-old South African fast bowler took 17 wickets for 86 runs and Somerset lost only their third match of the season.

So, it came down to the last match of the season and it would appear that this final match had been arranged by the cricket Gods, as the only two teams who could win the title were paired. Sadly, the weather intervened and Somerset were denied the opportunity to prove their might against the eventual champions, Essex.

The Royal London One Day Cup

RLODC   South Group 2019

TEAM		M	W	L	T	Pts
Hampshire	Q	8	7	1	0	14
Middlesex	Q	8	6	2	0	12
Somerset	Q	8	5	3	0	10
Gloucs		8	5	3	0	10
Sussex		8	4	4	0	8
Glamorgan		8	3	4	1	7
Kent		8	2	5	1	5
Essex		8	2	6	0	4
Surrey		8	1	7	0	2

Although Somerset only finished third in their group table, they eventually produced an all-round team performance in the Lord's final to lift their first piece of silverware in a few years. Their superlative team performance made Hampshire, who were the trophy winners in 2018, look like also-rans.

Tom Banton set them on their way with a truly masterful 69 from 67 balls and eventually it fell to the veteran James Hildreth to see Somerset across the line with an unbeaten half-century. Coincidentally, it was Hildreth who hit the winning runs when Somerset won the Twenty20 Cup in 2005, at the age of 20, which is Banton's age now.

Speaking to Andy in 2019, I asked him to elaborate on his seven years as Somerset 1st team Head Coach…

…and although he would challenge this assertion, it is beyond any doubt that the major changes that Andy introduced in 2007 and later with the help of Justin Langer, have proved their worth and paid dividends in the ensuing years.

One transformation that Andy is most proud of, is the recognition by other clubs, that in 2019 Somerset are the most professional County side in the country and how they have consistently been for many years.

References

Chapter 1

1 A History of the County of Middlesex: Volume 4

2 A History of Harrow School, 1324-1991. Christopher Tyreman

3 The court book of the barony of Urie in Kincardineshire 1604-1747. Various contributors

4 https://abertay.org.uk/wp-content/uploads/2017/08/CastleHuntly.pdf

5 Wikipedia https://en.wikipedia.org/wiki/Longforgan

6 Extracts from the Aberdeen & Commonwealth Line passenger list; SS Jervis Bay & SS Largs Bay

7 The Atlas of Living Australia http://www.ala.org.au

8 Welcome to Margaret River www.margaretriverwesternaustralia.com.au

9 The Atlas of Living Australia http://www.ala.org.au

10 An Economic History of Western Australia Since Colonial Settlement

11 http://www.abc.net.au/news/2014-02-26/100-years-of-drought/5282030

12 Immigration to Australia, 1901–39, Chapter 4. National Archives of Australia

References

13   https://www.rafmuseum.org.uk/about-us/our-history/Hendon-cradle-ofaviation.aspx

References

Chapter 2

[1] The Oxford English Dictionary

[2] London Directory of 1791

[3] Ship owners investing in the South Sea Whale Fishery from Britain: 1775-1815.

ISBN-10: 1526201364. ISBN-13: 978-1526201362

[4] http://www.origins.org.uk/genuki/NFK/norfolk/news papers/nfkchron/1780/08.s html#aug19)

[5] https://britishlistedbuildings.co.uk/101246591-133-king-street-great-yarmouthnelson-ward

[6] http://www.surnamedb.com/Surname/Hurry#ixzz581 vG3pfC

[7] https://www.houseofnames.com/hurry-family-crest

[8] https://www.engvid.com/english-resource/common-spelling-mistakes-inenglish/

References

Chapter 3

1. Publisher: Mercer University Press. ASIN: B01FJ01IKG

2. Nonconformists were people who did not belong to the established church. In England, up until 1533, this meant the Catholic Church, but that then changed when in 1559 the Act of Uniformity made the Church of England the established church. http://www.nationalarchives.gov.uk/help-with-yourresearch/research-guides/nonconformists/

3. The Barons of the Exchequer, or barones scaccarii, were the judges of the English court known as the Exchequer of Pleas. The Barons consisted of a Chief Baron of the Exchequer and several puisne (i.e. puny or junior) Barons.
   https://www.genguide.co.uk/source/guilds-freedoms-amp-freemens-orburgess-rolls-including-scotland/58/

References

1. Steve Tongue @stevetongue The Independent Newspaper Sunday 7 June 2009 00:00

2. ISBN: 1471130444: Publisher: Simon & Schuster UK; UK ed. edition (25 Sept. 2014)

3. http://www.givemesport.com/1174998-lewis-hamilton-from-child-star-tof1-legend

4. Seeing the Sunrise Main by Justin Langer (ISBN: 9781742371900)

5. http://www.bsecc.co.uk/club-history.html

6. Clark, Holly (and Red Van, photography). The Man behind the Pony Series, Finding My Father. Rusk, Texas: ClarkLand Productions, (Division of Phil Clark Foundation), 2006. ISBN 0-9785140-1-7.

7. https://hackney.gov.uk/hackney-marshes

References

1. https://www.royalnavy.mod.uk/careers/royal-marines

2. https://www.forces.net/news/cassidy-little-coming-home-afghanistan

Further reading

- A letter to Sir Francis Milman, Bart. M.D., President of the Royal College of Physicians of London, on the subject of the proposed reform in the condition of the apothecary and surgeon-apothecary: with an appendix, containing the correspondence between the general committee and the three corporate medical bodies by Kerrison, Robert Masters, 1776?-1847.
  Royal College of Surgeons of England.
  https://archive.org/details/b22323296
- https://www.artuk.org/discover/artists/opie-john-17611807 Of John Opie
- Popular Politics and the American Revolution in England: James E Bradley ISBN 086554-181-7
- Longforgan Conservation Area Appraisal Perth & Kinross Council.

Index

Index

Index

Index

Index

Index

Index

Index

Index

Index

Index

Index

Index

Notes

P129 The Capri was designed by American car designer Philip Clark as a European model almost identical to his earlier Mustang creation

P136 The Convent of Jesus and Mary was founded in 1860 after a group of French nuns moved into a small house on Orwell Road, Felixstowe and formed a day school in the house next to the church.

A year later, an orphanage was founded and 1862 saw the start of boarding. A new larger building opened in 1868 and the Convent of Jesus and Mary grew and prospered. Generations of girls and boys grew up under the caring and watchful eye of the nuns.

Times changed however, and in the 1980s, the school was closed and the convent rededicated to nuns in their retirement.

P146 The Falklands Islands, Islas Malvinas as the Argentines know them, are an isolated and sparsely populated British overseas territory in the south-west Atlantic Ocean. They remain the subject of a sovereignty dispute between Britain and Argentina, who waged a brief but bitter war over the territory in 1982. A British military task force ejected argentine forces, who had landed on the Falklands to stake a territorial claim.

Argentina says it has a right to the islands, because it inherited them from the Spanish crown in the early 1800s. It has also based its claim on the islands' proximity to the South American mainland. Britain rests its case on its long-term administration of the Falklands and on the principle of self-determination for the islanders, who are almost totally of British descent. The windswept and almost treeless territory is made up of two main islands, East Falkland and West Falkland, as well as hundreds of smaller islands and islets.7

There was considerable doubt and confusion at the top of the Government over how to respond to the noises emanating from Argentina. The Independent summarises it quite well in its article following the release of Thatcher's private papers in March 2013.

"Six months before the invasion of the Falkland Islands, British intelligence looked at the situation and – not for the last time – made a wrong call. "The Argentine government would prefer to pursue their sovereignty claim by peaceful means," they reported.

That unhelpful advice from the spooks is one of many revelations in the latest batch of Margaret Thatcher's private papers, released today, which also shed light on the political turmoil that the invasion created among Conservative MPs and the contradictory advice given to Mrs. Thatcher – ranging from a demand for blood to be spilt, to a suggestion that the islanders should be bribed generously to accept Argentine rule.

The top brass was happy to hear that they need not fear a military invasion of the islands, because they worried that they would not be able to get them back by force. "Such a deployment would be very expensive," a secret memo from the defence chiefs warned in September 1981. "Their geographical advantage and the relative sophistication of their armed forces would put our own task group at a serious disadvantage."

In January 1982, Mrs Thatcher wrote to the Tory MP Richard Needham, defending the decision to scrap the only British warship in the vicinity of the Falklands, HMS Endurance. The government needed to save money.

Three months later, with Endurance in the wrong place and the Falklands under Argentine occupation, Margaret Thatcher's government was plunged into, what contemporaries saw, as the worst overseas' crisis since the loss of the Suez Canal.

Over the next few days, Mrs. Thatcher received three memos from the Chief Whip, Michael Jopling, keeping her informed of how Tory MPs were reacting to the crisis. They ranged from "my constituents want blood", from the late Peter Mills, MP for Devon West, to "please no blood", from another MP, David Crouch – whereas the late Robert Rhodes James, historian turned Tory MP, was apparently "hopelessly defeatist, depressed and disloyal".

Kenneth Clarke, then a junior minister, said; ".... [he] hopes nobody thinks we are going to fight the Argentinians. We should blow up a few ships, but nothing more." One of his aides said: "His actual view was that he supported the invasion and very much hoped that there wasn't going to be a full-scale war with Argentina."

Notes

Chris Patten, chairman of the BBC Trust [in 2013], promised to "write a supportive article in the press once the situation is clearer".

Later, Jopling supplied a breakdown of the various factions forming within the party, from the "no surrender group" headed by Alan Clark, to "the Falkland Islands are not worth all this trouble" and "do not fire a shot in anger" groups, whose leader was the former Cabinet minister Sir Ian Gilmour, and whose members included Stephen Dorrell, now a senior backbench Tory, who was described as "wobbly".

Among the documents also released by the Margaret Thatcher Archive Trust are 22 pages of near-illegible notes taken by her parliamentary aide, Ian Gow, during an explosive meeting of backbench MPs the day after the invasion.

The members vented their anger at the Foreign Office, particularly the hapless minister Sir Humphrey Atkins, who was accused of giving wrong information to the Commons. He mistakenly told the House that an attack was not imminent; hours after Argentine troops had taken

Port Stanley. "How could even an office boy at the FO say this?" the MP John Carlisle demanded, to "prolonged cheers".

Under attack from fellow MPs and the newspapers, the then Foreign Secretary, Peter Carrington, and his two junior ministers promptly resigned. The papers show that Mrs. Thatcher did not want to lose Carrington and had to battle to keep her Defence Secretary, John Nott, from resigning as well. One of the ex-ministers, Richard Luce, had a self-justifying session with Gow a few days later, during which he claimed that a former Labour Foreign Secretary, George Brown, had told his Argentinian counterpart, that "Britain did not give a damn about the Falkland Islands".

If that were the considered Foreign Office view in the 1960s, it was not very different from the privately expressed views of some of Mrs. Thatcher's closest advisers. Alan Walters, her economic adviser, urged her to avoid conflict by getting Argentina to pay compensation to the islanders. "This jingo mood will pass," he forecast.

Notes

A lengthy memo from her Chief of Staff, David Wolfson, suggested the islanders be given a "US-backed guarantee" that if they did not like living under Argentine rule, they could at any time take British, Australian or New Zealand citizenship, and receive a resettlement grant equivalent to $100,000 per family, index-linked. Those closest to Mrs Thatcher also wondered how she could ever survive the crisis. Gow wrote to her on 8 April, six days after the invasion, to say that

"Whatever the future holds" he would always be glad he had had the chance to work with her. "It would be sad if Falkland precipitated the downfall of the

Thatcher government," her chief policy adviser, Sir John Hoskyns, wrote on the same day. Ten weeks later, the Falklands had been retaken, and Mrs. Thatcher was riding a surge of popular adulation. Congratulations poured in from around the world – although oddly there was none from EU governments.

However, she did receive – and seemingly appreciated – flowers from the Revolutionary Democratic Front of El Salvador, the political wing of a Cuban backed guerrilla army fighting to overthrow a US-backed dictatorship. The

Notes

Argentine junta had been the only South American government to lend troops to help suppress the guerrillas. The message that came with the flowers said: "You have succeeded where we failed. Since the dispatch of the Task Force to the Falkland Islands, 266 Argentine military advisers have been withdrawn from Central America. Thank you."

P286 Following the 1945 election, which resulted in a 146 seat majority for Labour under Clement Atlee, the 1950 election resulted in a massive swing to the Conservatives and Labour's majority was reduced to 5.

Various factors conspired to hinder the effective mechanism of the Labour Government so Atlee gambled on another snap election in 1951, which resulted in Churchill seizing the House of Commons with a 17 seat majority. History records that among other factors, the Conservatives, with many younger candidates than Labour appealed to the voters more.

Dartford, like many towns in the United Kingdom began to prosper in the 1950s. The National Health Service (NHS) had been implemented in 1948, which meant that for the first time, people could receive health treatment free of charge; society was changing though. The Dartford Archive records; "Youth culture began to emerge on the streets. Coffee bars began in Dartford. Teddy boys made an appearance on the streets with their own style of fashion and an arrogant disregard for authority. American rock 'n' roll music first hit Britain in the middle 1950s and skiffle music was popular in the town. There was a significant rise in petty crime throughout Dartford". 2 years National Service was still compulsory though.

Brian's father was in the RAF and he spent much of his very early life living on RAF Locking in Weston-Super-Mare (W-S-M) starting school at RAF Locking Primary School, then quite quickly he was sent to Locking Primary School then onto another RAF school. The family was then posted overseas to Singapore and Brian attended the Alexandra Barracks School on the south side of the Island.

Living in Singapore was; "...a joy..." and Brian recalls that as an 8 year old he would be at school by 7.30; school finished at 12.30 and he was picked up by an armoured truck, which had a sub-machine gun on the back. The country, at this time, was going through a period of change and insurrection and the families of servicemen were given special protection.

According to an article on the 'visit Singapore' website, in the 3rd Century ACE (formerly AD), the Chinese named the island "Pu-luo-chung", or the "island at the end of a peninsula". Later, the main city was known as Temasek ("Sea Town"), when the first settlements were established from ACE 1298-1299.

According to legend Singapore got its name from Sang Nila Utama, a Prince from Palembang (the capital of Srivijaya). He was out on a hunting trip when he caught sight of an animal he had never seen before. Taking it to be a good sign, he founded a city where the animal had been spotted, naming it "The Lion City" or Singapura, from the Sanskrit words "simha" (lion) and "pura" (city)

Modern Singapore was founded in the 19th century, thanks to politics, trade and a man known as Sir Thomas Stamford Raffles. There is still a Hotel called Raffles to this day.

Notes

During this time, the British Empire was looking for a base in this region; for its merchant fleet and to forestall any advance made by the Dutch. Singapore, already a growing trading post along the Malacca Straits, seemed ideal.

At the start of the Second World War, the Japanese were planning a raid on the island. Singapore subsequently surrendered to Japanese forces on 15th February 1942; Chinese New Year of the Horse.

P275 MIDDLESEX

Justin Langer (Alf or JL to his friends and colleagues) signed to play county cricket for Middlesex from 1998 to 2000, captaining the side in 2000. In his first season, he scored his maiden century in English domestic cricket in superb fashion; ironically, with 233 not out against Somerset at Lord's.

Somerset Lad (originally published in Last Word on Cricket)

JL signed for Somerset in July 2006, initially for six weeks. In the end, he remained with the club for three

Notes

years, assuming the captaincy from 2007, the year that Somerset won promotion to Division 1 after winning the second division by the huge margin of 52 points. Under JL's captaincy, Marcus Trescothick and Andrew Caddick featured in the leading averages for batting and bowling respectively.

In Somerset, JL and his family stayed in a rented house in Hatch Beauchamp, a village a couple of miles east of Taunton. Of Hatch Beauchamp (pronounced Beecham), he said; "Mate, I say this with the utmost affection and respect, but it's like living in the olden days".

On 20 July 2006, JL made his highest first-class score of 342 playing for Somerset in a County Championship match against Surrey at the Woodbridge Road ground in Guildford. This was also the highest score ever by a Somerset batsman, breaking the record of Sir Vivian Richards who made 322 against Warwickshire at Taunton.

Notes

During this six-week spell at Somerset, he also enjoyed particular success in the Twenty20 competition, topping the batting averages along with fellow Australian and Somerset overseas player Cameron White.

On 1 January 2007, he announced his retirement from Test cricket after the fifth Ashes Test against England, starting at the Sydney Cricket Ground the following day.

He wanted to continue to play first-class cricket in the English league and the announcements were synchronised to the world that he had agreed to return to Somerset in 2007 as captain. He had said during his retirement announcement that he was relishing the return to Somerset; saying; "There's an amazing challenge at Somerset and I've got a great regard for [Andy Hurry] the coach over there and I'm really looking forward to the challenge

On 20 April 2007, he became the first Somerset player to score two triple centuries in the County Championship when he hit 315 against Middlesex in a match noted for its extraordinary batting. Replying to the Middlesex first innings total of 600 runs, Somerset set a new record for the County Ground scoring a staggering 850 for 7 declared. At the close of the 2007 season, on 19 September Somerset announced that Langer would stay with them as captain for the 2008 season. In 15 first-class matches for the county in 2007, he scored 1215 runs at 57.85 and a further 764 runs in one-day competitions.

Notes

Further Reading: Dialects and Language Variations of Hurry

The surname Hurry has a long-recorded history and there are conflicting accounts of its heritage, with some scholars according it to be of English derivation, while others provide evidence of Scottish origins. There is also some evidence that it is of Old English (of Norman origin): from a Norman form of the Middle English personal name Wol(f)rich, but there appears to be a tacit agreement that it originated in the United Kingdom. (Courtesy of Name Origin Research 1980 – 2017:

http://www.surnamedb.com/Surname/Hurry)
Nevertheless, the name is certainly old, with the first recorded spelling of the family name believed to be that of Walter Urri. This was dated 1208, in the "Curia Regis" rolls of Lincolnshire, during the reign of King John, 1199 – 1216. There are other recorded examples as; Herueus Urri in the Pipe Rolls of the county of Norfolk in 1209, Alan Hurry in Essex in 1219 and a Geoffrey Orry in Salop in 1235, (Salop being the ancient name for Shropshire, the abbreviation of Anglo-Norman French Salopesberie, a corruption of Old English Scrobbesbyrig 'Shrewsbury).[1]

Notes

The first recorded use in Scotland, in Ayrshire is in 1260. One of the first records of the name was Adam Urri who appears as burgess of Irvine in 1260 and Huwe Urry of Ayrshire who rendered homage to King Edward I of England in his brief intrusion into Scotland in 1296. Reginald Urry held land in Irvine in 1323 and William Urri resigned the lands of Fulton in 1409. Another branch of the family lived in the Fetteresso parish, Kincardineshire and for the most part, these names included "de" denoting "of." Hugh de Urre swore fealty (sworn loyalty) at St. John of Perth and later with a different spelling as Hugh Uny at Forfar, 1296. [23]

As with most other names, there are variations such as Horrey, Hurry, Hurrey, Orry, Ourry, Urry, Uri and Urri. These can typically be traced back to

1. Differing dialects
2. Differing accents
3. Different spellings (e.g. phonetic spelling) and note that UK English is not classed as a phonetic language[4]
4. Limited literacy

Notes

1. As an example of different dialects, in the South East of England Brown is generally spoken with the diphthong OW sound whereas in the North and in Scotland it may be pronounced Broon with the diphthong OO sound. In fact, in 'the dialect of Robert Burns' by Sir Wilson James, James quotes Burns using the word Broon for the word Brown.

2. Some dialects don't pronounce a hard 'H' so in some parts of the country Hurry may be pronounced 'Urry or OOry, OOree or even OOray!

3. The word 'UP' is normally spoken with a hard 'U' in the South East but can be pronounced with the diphthong 'OO' the further north one goes.

4. Finally, although phonetics are generally associated with learning to speak, spell and write a language, it is common knowledge that people may be able to converse and understand each other through the medium of speech, but when it comes to the written word *and* when there is the added factor of an imperfect literacy, then confusion may reign.

Notes

For example, the phrase; "OK" stems from the words; "orl k'rrekt? "Thus, it may be the case that, although there are several different spellings of the name Hurry, they may ALL be just dialectal or accent variations on the one name.

---oOo---

Notes

Chapter 3

Further Reading: Root and Branch

Thanks in a large part to one of Andy's uncles, Uncle Sydney and further research and validation of certain facts by the author, it has been possible to trace the Hurry Family lineage to the mid-14th century. As with most families, the litany of names is extensive. The list of names, which grace the Hurry Family Tree - determined so far is-

Name	Possible origin
Brooks	Residing Near a Brook, From the Swedish surname Bäckland. Old Anglo-Saxon Origins
Brookes	Possibly an alternative spelling of Brooks
Butcher	From the Old English word Boucher; it may have Old French origins as in Bouchier.
Church	From the Old English pre-7th century "Cyrice" and Greek "Kyricaon" - house of the Lord.
Clifton	From the Old English - settlement by the cliff.

Notes

Cobb

From Cornwall about 1201 "Cobba" is derived from the term meaning "Lump"; both Old English and Old Norse terms used to denote a large, well built, man.

Dann

Anglo-Saxon Origin; a topographical name for a dweller in the valley, deriving From the Old English pre-7th century "Denu" meaning "valley".

Fowler

Of Anglo-Saxon Origin, and is from an occupational name for a bird-catcher, or hunter of wild birds. In the Medieval period, a fowler would have been an important position, and all major houses would have employed one. The derivation is from the Old English pre-7th century "Fugelere", i.e. hunter of wild birds. (from the modern German word for bird, vögel.)

Harrison

of early Medieval English origin. It is a form of the Medieval male given name Harry, itself a pet form of Henry; from the Latin Henricus", via the Old German "Haimric"; the names composed of the elements "Haim" meaning "Home", and "Ric" meaning "Power". By a similar route the Old French, and indeed the modern French is "Henri ".

Howlett

of Germanic origin; (Son of) Of Hugh. From the Old German personal name "Hugo", meaning heart or soul.

Hurry	H. Harrison, in " Surnames of the United Kingdom," Vol. I, page 223, says that Hurry (A-Fr-Tent.) has various forms: Hure, Hurey, Hury, and Hare, and means "Shaggy-Headed."
Ives	Derives from the Norman personal name "Ivo" and from the Old Norse "Yr", (Plural "Ifar"), meaning yew bow. A weapon made generally from the supple wood of the Yew tree.
McLaren	Scottish, from the pre-10th century "Mac (Son Of) Labhruinn"; originally the ancient Roman name Lawrence.
McNaughton Young	The derivation of the surname is ultimately from the pre-10th century Gaelic 'Mac' meaning son of, and the personal name Naughton or Naughten.
Meal	This surname is associated with the village of Meolse, Lancashire, which was recorded in the Domesday Book of 1086.
Moppett	Of Medieval English, meaning "little", or "son of" Mabb, itself a derivative of Amabel or Amabella, from the Latin "amabilis" meaning "the lovable one". In this case, the surname means the "son of

Mabb" or "Little Mabb", from Norman French.

Naughten	it is claimed, was of Ancient Gaelic mythology, the God of water and the sea
Neal	Of Gaelic origin where the name been Anglicised from the Gaelic Niall. The Gaelic name may be derived from words meaning cloud, passionate, or champion. (Maybe it is a corruption of Meal, or maybe *vice versa*.)
O'Neill	Derived from the Irish Gaelic the original elements of which, Ua and Néill, mean "grandson of Néill or Niall".
Park	The surname was first found In Cumberland, where the family held a family seat from early times. One of the first records of the name was when Rober De Parco witnessed a Charter by Earl David (C.1202-1207).
Porter	Of Old French origin, and has two possible sources; it may be an occupational name for the gatekeeper of a town; or it may be a doorkeeper of a large house. It derives from the Middle English "Porter", a development of the Old French "Portier". "…to carry" in modern French is "porter".
Rankin	Kin of (i.e. relating to) Ronald or Rand

Rust	Old English pre-7th century word meaning Red and it was given originally as a nickname to someone with reddish hair or a ruddy complexion
Scarfe	of Old Norse origin, and is found mainly in Northern England and Scotland, especially the Orkneys, and has two possible sources. The first source is locational from any of the various places named with the Old Norse topographical term "skarth", gap, notch. The second source is from the Old Norse byname "Skarthi", meaning hare-lipped, a derivative of "skarth", as before. Other sources quote it as a nickname from Old Norse for the Cormorant
Stewart	This famous clan surname is regarded as the Royal name of Scotland. It is however, arguably of Old English pre-7th century origins as it derives from the ancient word "Stigweard", then later Steward; a compound of "Stig" meaning household, and "Weard", a guardian. As such, it was the status and title used by an officer who controlled the domestic affairs of a royal or noble household.
Taylor	French and Latin Origin; Old French 'Tailleur' (Cutter)
Wright	Old French "Wrytte", Maker, Craftsman
Young	Middle English Yunge, Yonge; Younger Son

Notes

Trescothick

Marcus Trescothick, a handsome, tanned man of athletic build is Somerset through and through. He joined Somerset in 1992 as a seventeen-year-old and his precocious talent was evident from a young age when as a twelve-year-old, playing against adults at Lansdown and Downend cricket clubs, he would smash the ball to every corner of the ground. Marcus says; "I loved Lansdown because the wickets there always favoured the batsmen. I also enjoyed playing at Downend because it is such a tiny ground and it doesn't take much to hit the ball out of it." Typically, modest.

Marcus is an unassuming man, professional to the letter and a fine ambassador for the club. Andy will readily admit that there are certain people who have been major influences on him and one of these is Marcus. When Marcus retired from International cricket, he along with Justin Langer, Alf to his friends, were very supportive and Andy valued their cricketing brains and leadership skills.

Notes

Sitting in a busy Stragglers Bar inside the Cooper Associates County Ground, Marcus recalls the time that Somerset won the second division of the County Championship In 2007, under head coach Andy Hurry. " Included in that winning team were five international players, Marcus himself, Andy Caddick,

Justin Langer, Ian Blackwell and Charl Willoughby who had 225 test matches between them". The team also included a young Peter Trego, James Hildreth, Craig Kieswetter and the Australian Cameron White.

Justin Langer and Michael Vaughan are among a wealth of superb cricketers and sportsmen and women on record as saying that they thought Marcus was one of the best opening batters in the County and International game.

He is still one of the best considering the number of Somerset batting records he's broken over the years. He now graces our screens as one of the first-class expert commentators on SKY. I along with every single Somerset supporter am extremely proud of this great man.

Notes

Nasser Hussain will openly compliment Marcus' talents and his natural fit into the SKY team, his easy nature and vast experience of the game. Marcus is happy to acknowledge that there is a mutual admiration between the two of them.

As we're sitting drinking our coffee a couple of people come over and quickly say hello. Marcus is gracious and polite and says hello back; I ask him how he deals with well-wishers. He answers by talking about the time when watching football at Bristol City that a number of fans came over wanting to shake Marcus' hand and say hello.

He accepts it as "part and parcel" of his fame but he tells me that if he saw David Beckham in a room he'd be as star-struck. This just proves that no matter who we are we all have our champions and favourites.

Notes

Justin Langer

Picture: PerthNow, Richard Hatherly

Over the many years that Somerset CCC has been in existence, it has been variously, a Gentleman's club, an amateur club, and now professional club; it has also played host to several of the game's very best cricketers who proudly served as captain for the club.

The earliest of these was:

- **Sammy Woods**, an Australian who was captain in 1894.

and others include…

- **Rollo Meyer**   **the founder of Millfield School, a 'breeding ground' for so many Somerset's players, was captain in 1947.**

- **Colin Atkinson**   **another Millfield head & captain in 1961.**

- **Peter Wright**   **West Indian, in 1963**

- **Ian Botham**   **in 1980**

- **Viv Richards**   **West Indian, in 1981**

- **Mushtaq Ahmed**   **Pakistani in 1998**

- **Jamie Cox**   **Australian, in 1999**

- **Ricky Ponting**   **Australian in 2004**

- **Graeme Smith**   **South African, in 2005**

- **Cameron White**   **Australian, in 2006**

- **Justin Langer**   **Australian, in 2006**

- **Marcus Trescothick in 2010**

- **Alfonso Thomas**   **South African, in 2011**

- **Chris Rogers**   **Australian in 2016**

- **Tom Abell**   **in 2017**

- **Lewis Gregory**   **in 2019**

Notes

Other overseas players invited to play at Somerset in recent times include:

- **Chris Gayle**   the West Indian batter
- **Joel 'Big Bird' Garner** Barbadian fast bowler
- **Sanath Jayasuriya** Sri Lankan Captain
- **Aamer Sohail**   the Pakistani opener
- **Abdur Rehman**   the Pakistani all-rounder
- **Azhar Ali**   the Pakistani all-rounder
- **Piyush Chawla**   the Indian all-rounder
- **Sunil Gavaskar**   Indian opener

Notes

Lewis Gregory

Tom Abell

Notes

Notes

Notes

Notes

Notes

About the Author

Paul Nicholls, who writes under the pseudonym PJ Lennon, lives in the peaceful Somerset countryside in the beautiful town of Wiveliscombe (Wivey), a few miles west of Somerset's county town of Taunton and in sight of the Quantocks. Originally from Debden, in Essex, he spent many weekends as a youngster watching club cricket at Loughton Cricket Club and following Essex County Cricket Club at Valentines Park, Ilford and around the county and watching his favourite football team, West Ham United at the Boleyn Ground.

His love of journalism blossomed quite late in life, while sharing his love of music and broadcasting biographies on

10radio, a community radio station in Wivey. Combining this with his love of cricket, reporting firstly on Somerset County Cricket Club and progressing through to be the first community radio journalist to obtain his ECB and ICC accreditation and reporting on International cricket with the England team around the country.

Printed in Great Britain
by Amazon

47437318R00208